— *The* —
SINNER / SAINT DEVOTIONAL
• 60 DAYS IN THE PSALMS •

The SINNER / SAINT DEVOTIONAL
• 60 DAYS IN THE PSALMS •

EDITED BY
DANIEL EMERY PRICE

The Sinner/Saint Devotional: 60 Days in the Psalms
© 2018 Daniel Emery Price

All rights reserved. No part of this publication may be reproduced, distributed, or transmitted in any form or by any means, including photocopying, recording, or other electronic or mechanical methods, without the prior written permission of the publisher, except in the case of brief quotations embodied in critical reviews and certain other noncommercial uses permitted by copyright law. For permission requests, write to the publisher at the address below.

Published by:
1517 Publishing
PO Box 54032
Irvine, CA 92619-4032

Cover design by Brenton Clarke Little

Printed in the United States of America

Publisher's Cataloging-In-Publication Data
(Prepared by The Donohue Group, Inc.)

Names: Price, Daniel Emery, editor, contributor. | Wilson, Jared C., 1975- contributor. | Van Voorhis, Daniel, 1979- writer of supplementary textual content.
Title: The sinner/saint devotional : 60 days in the Psalms / edited by Daniel Emery Price ; [[contributors], Jared C. Wilson [and 10 others] ; intro by: Daniel Van Voorhis].
Other Titles: Sinner saint devotional
Description: Irvine, CA : 1517 Publishing, [2018]
Identifiers: ISBN 9781962654913 (IPG: softcover) | 9781945978753 (softcover) | 9781945978760 (hardcover) | 9781945978777 (ebook)
Subjects: LCSH: Bible. Psalms.—Meditations. | Bible. Psalms.—Devotional use. | Devotional exercises.
Classification: LCC BS1430.54 .S56 2018 (print) | LCC BS1430.54 (ebook) | DDC 242/.5—dc23

Unless otherwise stated, all scripture has been taken from the ESV® Bible (The Holy Bible, English Standard Version®). ESV® Text Edition: 2016. Copyright © 2001 by Crossway, a publishing ministry of Good News Publishers. The ESV® text has been reproduced in cooperation with and by permission of Good News Publishers. Unauthorized reproduction of this publication is prohibited. All rights reserved.

Scripture taken from *The Message*. Copyright © 1993, 1994, 1995, 1996, 2000, 2001, 2002. Used by permission of NavPress Publishing Group.

CONTENTS

INTRODUCTION
The Psalms, Prayer and our Communal Devotional Life xi
By Daniel Van Voorhis

DAY 1 PSALM 71:3
God's Command to Save You 1
By Bruce Hillman

DAY 2 PSALM 122:1
I'm Not Always Glad to Go to the House of the Lord 3
By Chad Bird

DAY 3 PSALM 46:2
Jesus in the Heart of the Sea 5
By Cindy Koch

DAY 4 PSALM 2:1–12
Kiss the Son 8
By Elyse Fitzpatrick

DAY 5 PSALM 118:17
I Will Not Die, But I Will Live 12
By Donavon Riley

DAY 6 PSALM 139:19–22
God's Enemies? 15
By Erick Sorensen

DAY 7 PSALM 115:1
Our Hearts before God's Throne 18
By Jessica Thompson

DAY 8 PSALM 3
Salvation Belongs to the Lord 20
By Joel Fitzpatrick

DAY 9 PSALM 23:6
Hunted by Goodness and Mercy — 23
By Daniel Emery Price

DAY 10 PSALM 1:5–6
The True Man — 25
By Jared C. Wilson

DAY 11 PSALM 104:24
Asking and Thanking — 28
By Steven Paulson

DAY 12 PSALM 22:6
Don't Ignore the Worm — 31
By Cindy Koch

DAY 13 PSALM 51:3–4
Ill-Conceived: Pinpointing When Our Lives Went Wrong — 34
By Chad Bird

DAY 14 PSALM 32:1–2
Will God Forgive Me . . . Again? — 37
By Bruce Hillman

DAY 15 PSALM 8:3–4
Tiny, Weak, and Cared For — 39
By Elyse Fitzpatrick

DAY 16 PSALM 130:1
You Are Not Forgotten — 42
By Donavon Riley

DAY 17 PSALM 34:8
Taste The Goodness — 45
By Erick Sorensen

DAY 18 PSALM 131:2
Becoming Like Weaned Children — 47
By Jessica Thompson

DAY 19 PSALM 4
Ugly Prayer and the God of Sleep — 49
By Joel Fitzpatrick

DAY 20 PSALM 51:7
You Are Not as White as Snow — 53
By Daniel Emery Price

DAY 21 PSALM 24:1–2
The Shape of Gospel Astonishment — 56
By Jared C. Wilson

DAY 22 PSALMS 9 & 10
The Hidden God and My Hiding Place — 58
By Steven Paulson

DAY 23 PSALM 1:3
Planted in His Garden — 61
By Cindy Koch

DAY 24 PSALM 22:1
My God, My God, Why Have You _____ Me? — 64
By Chad Bird

DAY 25 PSALM 112:6–8
Anxious, Fearful, and Righteous — 67
By Bruce Hillman

DAY 26 PSALM 27:4
Gazing at the Goodness of Another — 69
By Elyse Fitzpatrick

DAY 27 PSALM 37:12
Shooting at the Sun — 72
By Donavon Riley

DAY 28 PSALM 32:3–5
Keeping Heavy Secrets — 75
By Erick Sorensen

DAY 29 PSALM 25
The God of Rejects — 78
By Jessica Thompson

DAY 30 PSALM 117
Blurting Out Praise — 80
By Joel Fitzpatrick

DAY 31 PSALM 116:7
The Lost Art of Rest — 83
By Daniel Emery Price

DAY 32 PSALM 51:1
What Sin? — 86
By Steven Paulson

DAY 33 PSALM 147:12–18
The Word that Melts the Cold — 89
By Cindy Koch

DAY 34 PSALM 23
The Lord Is My Shepherd, but I Still Want — 92
By Chad Bird

DAY 35 PSALM 142:1–3A
God, I'm Mad at You — 94
By Bruce Hillman

DAY 36 PSALM 56:3
Fear and Trust, Hand-in-Hand — 96
By Elyse Fitzpatrick

DAY 37 PSALM 147:11
The Lord's Favor Is On You — 99
By Jared C. Wilson

DAY 38 PSALM 19:1–3
The Heavens Declare the Glory of God (and That's Not Enough) — 101
By Erick Sorensen

DAY 39 PSALM 65:1–4
Coming to the God Who Hears — 105
By Jessica Thompson

DAY 40 PSALM 133
Unity Like Beard Oil — 107
By Joel Fitzpatrick

DAY 41 PSALM 14:1
Overcoming Our Foolish Hearts — 110
By Daniel Emery Price

DAY 42 PSALM 48
What the People of God Will Be (and Are!) — 112
By Jared C. Wilson

DAY 43 PSALM 33:1–12
He Preached, and It Stood Firm — 115
By Steven Paulson

DAY 44 PSALM 119:1–3
Blameless and Blessed — 119
By Cindy Koch

DAY 45 PSALM 88
Prayers Splashed with the Blood of the Cross   **123**
By Chad Bird

DAY 46 PSALM 127:2
You Can't Work for Peace   **126**
By Bruce Hillman

DAY 47 PSALM 19:7, 14
The Restored Soul   **129**
By Elyse Fitzpatrick

DAY 48 PSALM 45:7
Sinners Who Love Righteousness   **132**
By Donavon Riley

DAY 49 PSALM 13:1–2
Venting (to the Glory of God)   **135**
By Erick Sorensen

DAY 50 PSALM 143:8
What We Need, Every Day   **138**
By Jessica Thompson

DAY 51 PSALM 30:4–5
Dancing with God   **140**
By Joel Fitzpatrick

DAY 52 PSALM 144:7–11
We Will Out-Sing the Enemy   **143**
By Jared C. Wilson

DAY 53 PSALM 78:4
The Hard and Wonderful Deeds of God   **145**
By Cindy Koch

DAY 54 PSALM 34
What a Madman Teaches Us about Prayer in Chaotic Times   **148**
By Chad Bird

DAY 55 PSALM 2:1
When Jesus Comes Close   **151**
By Donavon Riley

DAY 56 PSALM 5:7
You Are Welcome Here   **154**
By Elyse Fitzpatrick

DAY 57 PSALM 145:14
Jesus and Troubled Waters **157**
By Erick Sorensen

DAY 58 PSALM 103:3
Forget Not All His Benefits **159**
By Jessica Thompson

DAY 59 PSALM 118:26
Welcome Home **162**
By Donavon Riley

DAY 60 PSALM 140:7
A Helmet of Promises **165**
By Bruce Hillman

MEET THE AUTHORS **169**

INTRODUCTION

THE PSALMS, PRAYER AND OUR COMMUNAL DEVOTIONAL LIFE

By Daniel Van Voorhis

Our view of prayer can be far too pious—especially if you see prayer as merely a pious exercise in polite requests, canned praise, a wink, and maybe a wish. And if bringing the right attitude and proper mood of contemplation and sorrow is a prerequisite for prayer, the psalmist is giving us a lousy example. The Psalms are emotionally bipolar, from one high to the depths of despair. But the Psalms are not the journaling of a tortured young Jewish poet. The Psalms are the communal prayer book of the Bible. They are, of course, many things, but we do well in our age to remember them primarily as a communal work of prayer as opposed to merely private. There need not be an argument for the individual reading and interpretation of the Psalms as we have, since Gutenberg, become masters at the personal and private. But these are not necessarily the tame, communal prayers you may be used to. If you think of prayer as something done quietly with head bowed, hands folded, and eyes squeezed shut, the Psalms might seem a little over emotional, maybe a little charismatic, self-righteous, or possibly morose for you.

If we don't see these as actually emotive prayers, they can lead indirectly to a lazy exegesis that has little role for the variances of human perception and emotion. Are these the words of God? David? The Psalmist? Yes. What do we do with those almost painfully self-righteous Psalms wherein the author confirms his own righteousness in the face of his oppressors despite clear texts elsewhere in the Bible that you should not do that? The psalmist sometimes claims a righteousness that seems far too pure. Furthermore, the Psalms are irreverent and emotional. The Psalms are "too" pessimistic about human ability to stand up against injustice, they seem "too" self-righteous, as well as "too" comfortable playing with broad categorizations of people as good or evil.

LAW, GOSPEL, AND THE PSALMS

The Lutheran distinction of Law and Gospel is of indescribable help when faced with doubt, sin, and death (which, frankly, is most of the time for me). But it can be abused if taken, in a simplistic manner, and this is especially true with the Psalms. A quick primer: when we write of "Law," we mean anything that prohibits and condemns. Obviously, the Ten Commandments are the easy exhibition of this. But what of Christ's call to "be perfect"? On the Sermon on the Mount Jesus is not suggesting that we've all fallen short by a few percentage points. Rather, Christ tells us "you've heard it said, well . . . it's harder than that." Half measures don't do anything. Or take the rich young ruler in the gospels who tells Jesus, "Yup, I've done everything I am supposed to have done since my youth." Jesus's response seems at first unfair. "Great! So now sell everything you have and give it to the poor." It is a nice sentiment. But if that guy has already done everything he was supposed to do, shouldn't he get a pass?

It's not that easy, of course. I am sure that if the rich young man had actually done everything he was supposed to do, Jesus wouldn't have given him the extra assignment. Rather, face to face with the law ("sell all you have"), the young man walked away in despair. Jesus didn't take a pious and fresh-faced young man who had hitherto been sinless and dash his hopes. Rather, Jesus wields the law in such a way that no one can possibly say, "I've done it all." Gospel, on the other hand, is that which freely gives away. Passages like "Fear not little flock, it is the father's good intention to give you the kingdom of heaven," do not prohibit, condemn, cajole, ask, etc. The one way saving of his people is the real work of Christ. He came to condemn or forgive depending on how you have approached him. The rich young ruler takes the law and claims to have followed it, and thus Jesus points him to more law in a reminder to him that nothing can be kept perfectly. The man asks for the law (what else do I have to do?), and Jesus gives it to him. But what of the centurion whose daughter just died? The woman with medical issues? The thief on the cross?

Take any declarative statement in the Bible and ask yourself, "Is this telling me what to do or telling me what has been done?" Sure, once the gospel is preached in its fullest you-can-do-nothing-to-save-yourself goodness, we are reminded that we now walk in the light of this truth and need not go back to our old ways. But what happens, as a Christian, when I am told "therefore . . ." and I realize that I have not been loving God and my neighbor, walking in the fruit of the Spirit, etc.? I see then even those "therefore" statements as Law, and I run, don't walk, to a passage wherein I am reminded of what has been done for me. When I start to believe that, good works follow. If you aren't in particular Lutheran circles, this might seem simple. Don't worry—at our worst, we Lutherans tend to make it more complicated than it is. For instance, Johann Arndt, a sixteenth-century reformer, was asked to make this distinction between Law and Gospel with the crucifixion as his text. Is the crucifixion a story primarily of gospel or law? To answer this, you have to remember that the answer will depend on what relation the hearer has with the text and the good news of Christ's death for the sins of the world. If upon hearing the story you find a chord of terror has been struck within you and the bloody death of Christ serves as a reminder of just how seriously God takes sin, this would be categorized under "law" as it has turned into an injunction against sin. But if that same story brings you to see what has happened *on your behalf,* then the message is simply proclaiming, "Look what happened to your sins! They died with Jesus. They can't condemn you anymore." This is gospel.

If you're familiar with the law-gospel distinction, this might seem quite rudimentary to you. You ask, "What does the text say? How am I responding to it?" And then even when you get to the tricky "therefore" statements (sometimes referred to as the "third use of the law"), you can find both a deadly challenge and a promised rest in the words of scripture.

However, this seems almost impossible with the Psalms without doing torturous exegetical gymnastics.

As an educated, Western, and modern man, I like to deal with propositions. You tell me something that could be true or false, and I get to working out which it is. You might say "the light post is blue," which I confirm or deny. But what if you say, "The light post makes me sad"? We've left the world of propositions and are dealing in the affective domain. Unlike confirming the color of something we could all see for ourselves, your feelings are not discoverable by others as true or false. Even if you are sure that the person doesn't actually feel what they say they feel, a rational conversation about the veracity of the feeling isn't likely to go anywhere. Take for instance a very real issue in my household. There is no way my wife can be as hot as she claims every night when she's trying to sleep. The fan pushes an arctic breeze toward her side of the bed, and the sheets can't even touch her person. It is always seventy degrees in our house (thanks to the magic of Southern California and our cooling system). It is demonstrably not hot. Tell that to my wife.

Likewise, the psalmist seems to trade in the world of nonconfirmable feelings. Sure, someone could check to see if the psalmist's bed is actually wet with tears. Or if the psalmist actually thinks he is *that* beset upon by his enemies.

Old Testament scholar Walter Brueggeman has suggested that we read the Psalms as hymns of orientation (e.g., wow, I am observing some pretty amazing things), of disorientation (e.g., everything that seemed to be going okay is now going terribly wrong), and of reorientation (e.g., things seemed bad from my perspective, but remembering God's promises reminds me otherwise). Brueggeman suggests that the same psalm might be all three things to different people, and with that, we can tie the Psalms back into our Law/gospel schema. If I hear people talking about how mighty the ocean is, I start to agree and swear to never get on a boat again. These people might love the ocean and are marveling at its beauty, while the exact same description terrifies me. Sometimes the Psalms are pretty recognizable as "orienting" or "disorienting," but the reader is able to personalize the Psalms even in a communal setting. Take for instance Psalm 24:1-6:

> **The earth is the Lord's and the fullness thereof, the world and those who dwell therein, for he has founded it upon the seas and established it upon the rivers. Who shall ascend the hill of the Lord? And who shall stand in his holy place? He who has clean hands and a pure heart, who does not lift up his soul to what is false and does not swear deceitfully. He will receive blessing from the Lord and righteousness from the God of his salvation. Such is the generation of those who seek him, who seek the face of the God of Jacob.**

Brueggeman classifies this psalm as a hymn of orientation. Your eye may have darted to the requirements for being on the "hill of the Lord," and you might despair over your lack of clean hands. But those verses seem to affirm the general order of things (in the end good guys win, bad guys lose). It isn't jaded, demanding, or helpless but rather glorifies in the created order of God. Everything belongs to God, he has created everything, and those who do right will certainly find favor with him. It might sound Pollyannaish for the weary traveler of life's darker roads. But regardless of what the Psalms might later insist, this is also true. When we marvel at a sunset on an otherwise lousy day, we affirm the basic orientation of creation pointing toward its creator. Is it duplicitous to affirm the beauty of creation but also the gritty reality of a world askew? The psalmist doesn't think so. In fact, movement from these hymns of orientation to disorientation happen frequently.

> **As a deer pants for flowing streams, so pants my soul for you, O God. My soul thirsts for God, for the living God. When shall I come and appear before God? My tears have been my food day and night, while they say to me all the day long, "Where is your God?" These things I remember, as I pour out my soul: how I would go with the throng and lead them in procession to the house of**

> God with glad shouts and songs of praise, a multitude keeping festival. (Psalm 42:1-4)

These are not the rantings of a jaded person standing outside the congregation of the faithful but rather of one who once led the procession into the temple, whose ecstasy has turned to despair. And while this kind of soul-bearing is not foreign to the Bible, the psalmist allows the feeling of abandonment to sit (maybe even fester) and have the last word. We often see reference to the first verse in lush, pastoral settings, but it is clear that it is not a gentle or polite longing for flowing streams. The overall tone of hopefulness is achieved, however, with those Psalms we can classify as psalms of reorientation. Psalm 145 serves as a good example:

> I will extol you, my God and King, and bless your name forever and ever. Every day I will bless you and praise your name forever and ever. Great is the Lord, and greatly to be praised, and his greatness is unsearchable. One generation shall commend your works to another, and shall declare your mighty acts. On the glorious splendor of your majesty, and on your wondrous works, I will meditate. They shall speak of the might of your awesome deeds, and I will declare your greatness. They shall pour forth the fame of your abundant goodness and shall sing aloud of your righteousness. The Lord is gracious and merciful, slow to anger and abounding in steadfast love. The Lord is good to all, and his mercy is over all that he has made. All your works shall give thanks to you, O Lord, and all your saints shall bless you! They shall speak of the glory of your kingdom and tell of your power, to make known to the children of man your mighty deeds, and the glorious splendor of your kingdom. Your kingdom is an everlasting kingdom, and your dominion endures throughout all generations. (Psalm 145:1-13)

This psalm of reorientation takes the long view and recognizes that despite sometimes seeming otherwise, God is good. Despite the bitter complaining and the silent periods, we know God to be gracious and merciful. Taken in the Christian context, one can see what reorienting event leads us to say this. But we must not assume the daily graces and benevolence God shows us, he somehow failed to show his people then. The reorienting of the psalm reminds the community that the radical work of God on their behalf has taken a fallen world and will ultimately restore everything in the new heavens and earth.

Depending on where you find yourself, you might resonate more with a psalm of disorientation and will find deep meaning in them, but they cannot be your sole diet. It might be helpful to be around Christians of other dispositions, even if it is uncomfortable. I was recently at an underground church in Havana, Cuba, in a destitute part of town. Despite seeming run down in my eyes, the church was the loudest, most boisterous and energetic group I have ever been among. And it was incredibly uncomfortable. But I appreciated their thankfulness for seemingly so little. I understood their culture as inherently musical, and I witnessed the passion with which they sing about anything. I am of a disposition inclined toward Psalms of disorientation and thus must read those others that affirm the order of things as they can and will be. Individualism isn't lacking in this culture, and thus we do well to remind ourselves that all of the Bible, but specifically the Psalms, are meant to be read and experienced in community. And even in the midst of your sometimes stodgy coreligionists, it is okay to be moved by the emotion that accompanies the truths that might not always be as knowable or verifiable as we would like. We might feel disoriented, but the love of Yahweh for his sometimes-wayward people is absurd like that.

DAY 1

GOD'S COMMAND TO SAVE YOU

By Bruce Hillman

Be to me a rock of refuge to which I may continually come. You have given the command to save me, for you are my rock and my fortress.
—Psalm 71:3

In the gospel stories, there were a few occasions when Jesus was surprised. Think about that for a second. What does it take to surprise God? One of those stories is of the centurion, a Roman military officer who, via a messenger, begged Jesus to come to his home and heal his beloved servant (Luke 7:1-10). Jesus made his way to the home but was met somewhere along the way by another servant. This servant brought an updated message from the centurion, essentially telling Jesus to turn around and go home. The officer realized that Jesus's physical presence was not necessary for him to issue commands. His military background showed him all that was needed was the command, not Jesus's actual physical presence. Jesus marveled at his faith, for the centurion grasped what many in Jesus's inner circle were still struggling to understand: that his word is power.

God's word is always a promise to us, a revelation of God's will, intentions, and faithfulness. It is not just informative, giving us interesting information. It is primarily *covenantal*, expressing God's relational integrity and love for us. Sometimes God's promises take on a heightened intensity, like in this verse. We hear a promise in the form of a divine command: "You have given the command to save me." The motivation of this command follows: "For you are my rock and fortress." Why has God given such a command? Because he has already previously promised to be our safe place, our fortress.

The Psalmist opens with a wish that God would be for him a rock and refuge in which he may continuously come. And no sooner does he express his desire than he is reminded that God has already taken the first step. God has *already* acted first. He has *given a command to save me*.

While there are salvific implications for this verse (for God has saved us in Christ), the immediate context is not about eternal salvation but life's troubles. It is all well and good to be saved from sin and have eternal life with God. But how can my faith last and stay strong amid the troubles and hardships of life's daily surprises unless God is also with me *through to the end?* And he is!

The promise here is that God is present with us in our troubles, issuing commands to save us before we ask. God does not ignore our suffering and cries. Rather, he has already acted to save us from sin, death, and hell but also to be a place of safety for us in life's hardest moments. Because of God's first love for us, because God has chosen to save us, because God has made himself our fortress, God has commanded that he himself will rescue us in troubles. This is true. It is the divine command. It is not based on your piety but His promise. Let us live in this promise.

DAY 2

I'M NOT ALWAYS GLAD TO GO TO THE HOUSE OF THE LORD

By Chad Bird

I like the Psalms, but I can't pray some of them with a straight face. Psalm 122:1 is a prime example. David is a little too gung-ho for me as he exclaims, "I was glad when they said to me, 'Let us go to the house of the Lord!'"

That certainly doesn't roll off my tongue when I roll out of bed on Sunday morning. Maybe my wife and I stayed out late on Saturday night. There's still yard work and grocery shopping and laundry and a hundred other things that need to be done before Monday comes around. I'm likely to get corned by Mr. Meddler or Mrs. Gossipalot and have to find a way politely to excuse myself from them. Or maybe I'm just bone tired. I want to chill. I want to revel in my introversion. I just want to stay home on Sunday morning, drink coffee, and work hard at doing zilch. I'm not always smiling at the thought of going to the house of the Lord.

What may surprise you is that pastors don't always want to go to church, either. Maybe between sermon and Bible study preparations; hospital visits; committee meetings; counseling sessions; visitor follow-ups; late-night phone calls; and typing, copying, and folding the bulletins, they've worked their butts off the last six days. They could really use a day at the beach or a long walk in the park. They've tried to write a good sermon, but in all honesty, the one today is a total flop.

Honestly, some Sunday mornings, they wish they'd chosen a different vocation. For once, they'd like to leave their alarm clock unset on Sunday morning, sleep till the sun's up, and do nothing but be lazy. The last thing they'd pray is, "I was glad when they said, 'Let us go to the house of the Lord!'" What would make them very glad, however, is to stay at their own house, in bed.

I'm not saying every Sunday, or even most Sundays, are like this. Nor am I saying that this is true of every pastor—though I suspect most of them have been here more than they'd care to admit. But for many, there are days when they're as excited about going to work on Sunday morning as the rest of us are about going to work on Monday morning.

But here's the point: they go anyway. Glad or not, willing or not, they get out of bed and get themselves to the house of the Lord. And in so doing, in a most unexpected way, they fulfill another duty of their office: setting an example for their flocks.

No one, pastors or laypeople, goes to the house of the Lord for entirely pure, selfless, God-loving motives. We're all deeply flawed humans, with inflated egos, thin skin, lust-fat hearts, selfish ambitions, and plenty of other nastiness hidden beneath our Sunday best.

And for all those reasons, going to church is the best thing we can do, regardless of our motives. Because in church we'll hear about the God who loves us despite us flaws, who calls us to repentance, and who stands ready to wash us in the waters of forgiveness. We'll hear the good news of the Christ who died and rose for us, Mr. Meddler, Mrs. Gossipalot, and all others. We will kneel at the altar and hear Christ say, "Take, eat, this is my body," without ever questioning what our motives are for kneeling there. In the house of the Lord, the Spirit will apply the cleansing blood of Jesus to our hearts that are full of bad, twisted, and self-serving motives, so that our hearts are pumped full of nothing but the pure, saving blood of Christ.

When someone exclaims, "Let us go to the house of the Lord!" are we glad? Sometimes, yes. Sometimes, no. But one thing is certain: the Lord is glad to have us there. Always, without exception. And that's really all that matters. Because if he's there, he's there with love and absolution and a smile of grace on his face. We are his children. He's always overjoyed to see us. And when we leave his house, we leave with hearts overflowing with the mercy he has showered upon us in Jesus Christ.

DAY 3

JESUS IN THE HEART OF THE SEA

By Cindy Koch

Therefore, we will not fear though the earth gives way, though the mountains be moved into the heart of the sea.
—Psalm 46:2

The sky grows dark and angry. Rain drips, drips, drips, one heartbeat at a time, as the wind grows more violent by the minute. Thick black clouds now cover overhead, and the heavens all at once drench the earth below. Night and day, the horrible storm does not pass. Water builds and builds, filling every low place. Thunder shakes every tree, and lightning cracks. Waves from the shoreline below advance upon the dry places. Puffing up stronger and higher, the terrible surf devours the land. The sturdy, strong mountains begin to crumble. They shake and slide and change the very face of God's creation. Mountains, mighty and strong, sink deep into the forgotten recess of the sea.

Mother scrambles to collect her children as those awful waters pound at her dry and comfortable home. Father prepares for battle, mapping out the escape route to higher ground. Children sob in the shadows, frightened by the sounds and screams and the roaring waters that will not stop. And all the while, the earth is shaken out from under those who live there.

And there is nowhere to go. Every road collides into another dead end. Every plan slips closer to the advancing watery march of death. Cars and boats, highways and trails, the escapes of men are all shaken into the water. Kindness and love give way to survival as they are all pressed deep into the heart of the sea. Swallowing every good thing they thought they knew about each other. Devouring every hope they had in their own hands. Drowning every safe place that kept them blind to this destruction for so long. Tottering, gasping, dying in the raging sea. When God finally speaks his word, it all melts away.

As terrifying as the deadly, uncontrollable waters rage, as loud and persuasive as the angry world screams, as frantically as they cling to their own tumbling towers of trust, you will not fear. Even in the dying and the drowning and the changing of everything they hold dear, you will not fear. In the confusion and sadness and depression, you will not fear because God, who will never be shaken, is your refuge and our strength.

Stillness hovers over the water that smothered that blind and deaf, wicked generation upon the earth. The deep, watery grave now glimmers from the east. It is a brilliant glassy sea, sparkling like a diamond in the morning sun. Here a calm, gentle water flows from a river to a stream, which quenches a new City of Life. No more terrible sea. No more raging waters. Instead, a river of life remains for the healing of the nations. Here, God shines brightly in the middle of this blessed, beautiful place. Here, this city, these mountains, and this generation will never be shaken.

And you will not fear because the judgment flood already washed over your head when you were buried deep with Christ. United with Him in death, you have been violently shaken into the heart of the sea. But you will not fear because the healing waters already washed over your heart and you are raised up to live in the eternal City of God.

> **Do you not know that all of us who have been baptized into Christ Jesus were baptized into his death? We were buried therefore with him by baptism into death, in order that, just as Christ was raised from the dead by the glory of the Father, we too might walk in newness of life. For if we have been united with him in a death like**

> **his, we shall certainly be united with him in a resurrection like his. (Romans 6:3–5)**

For you, my friend, Christ is your only strength. He alone brought you back from death into his new life. His sacrifice was complete, not yours. His work was pleasing to his Father, not yours. His steady ground is where you now stand, not your own. No matter what comes, little or big, insignificant or tragic, mountains crumbling and floods raging, this peaceful City of God is your sure and solid promise. You will not get there by cleverness or wealth. You will not find it by avoiding the wickedness that crumbles all around. You are promised this everlasting city through death: death and destruction of the earth around us; death and destruction of your own desires; death and destruction of the holy Son of God, who perfectly tottered, sinlessly shook, righteously melted into the sea *for you*.

God truly is your only refuge. Christ Jesus alone is your strength. Therefore, you will not fear though the earth gives way, though the mountains be moved into the heart of the sea.

DAY 4

KISS THE SON

By Elyse Fitzpatrick

Why do the nations rage and the peoples plot in vain? The kings of the earth set themselves, and the rulers take counsel together, against the Lord and against his Anointed, saying, "Let us burst their bonds apart and cast away their cords from us." He who sits in the heavens laughs; the Lord holds them in derision. Then he will speak to them in his wrath, and terrify them in his fury, saying, "As for me, I have set my King on Zion, my holy hill." I will tell of the decree: The Lord said to me, "You are my Son; today I have begotten you. Ask of me, and I will make the nations your heritage, and the ends of the earth your possession. You shall break them with a rod of iron and dash them in pieces like a potter's vessel." Now therefore, O kings, be wise; be warned, O rulers of the earth. Serve the Lord with fear, and rejoice with trembling. Kiss the Son, lest he be angry, and you perish in the way, for his wrath is quickly kindled. Blessed are all who take refuge in him.
—Psalm 2:1-12

Have you ever tried to train a puppy to walk on a leash? I have, and I can tell you, it's not an easy task. No matter their size, they really hate the thought of anyone leading them by the neck to a place they don't want to go. They throw their heads back and forth and try to squirm out of the collar. They bite the leash and yelp like someone is torturing them. When we've been in the process of having to train a dog to walk on a leash, frequently we've said (only half-jokingly), "I'm going to go take the dog for a drag down the street." Whether the puppy wants to go or not, he's headed for the sidewalk, and his resistance is actually laughable. *Silly puppy*, we think, *you really aren't smart enough or strong enough to get away from me . . . and because I love you and want you to be part of our family, I'm going to teach you how to do this. You'll end up loving it (and me!) before long.*

Puppies hate being forced to walk on a leash. But they're not the only ones who hate being told what to do and who try in vain to throw off restraints. We delight in the deception that we're the captains of our ship, the masters of our fate. By nature, we really hate it if someone tries to tell us that we're not the one in charge or that someone else will be making decisions for us.

In Psalm 2, a song about the coronation of a king, we hear the voice of people who sound like those little puppies. They "rage" and "plot" against the king: *"You're not going to tell us what to do! Who made you the boss anyway?"* they shout. They want to throw off the restraints the king is putting on them. And in the same way we chuckle at that little fuzz ball thinking he'll get the upper hand, the king laughs at the futility of their vain attempts: "He who sits in the heavens laughs" (v. 4).

Initially David must have thought he was writing about the coronation of an earthly king, perhaps even himself. But as he continued to compose this song, suddenly he found that he was writing about something—Someone—else. He discovered that he was writing about an Anointed One and not merely talking about the ritual anointing that any earthly king would receive. No, he found that he had moved beyond that shadow and was referring to a Messianic King, a Christ (which is what that word *anointed* actually means).

This Psalm is essentially a song about Jesus the Christ, our Anointed One. It's a song about the One who will bring forgiveness and redemption to every proud, defiant heart who has shaken a fist at a sovereign or squirmed in vain to try to get free of his grip.

How does the Lord respond to these rebellious people? He will "speak to" and "terrify" them "in his wrath." Should we expect anything else? Everyone knows that mutiny triggers wrath. And yet . . . notice what the king says next: Instead of proclaiming, "Off with their heads!" he declares, "I have set my King on Zion, my holy hill." Instead of declaring our doom, he announces the Anointed One's coronation, our salvation. He has enthroned his King on Zion, his holy hill. He has done it. This was his plan from the very beginning, and the Lord will accomplish his plan, no matter how we might rage against it . . . or him. Jesus, the Anointed One, is Zion's King!

How does he change us from foolish, powerless rebels into meek, joyful servants? Not by pouring out his wrath on us but by pouring it out on Zion's King. He sends us the Messiah, the Anointed One who will take our punishment, the sentence we deserve. And he'll do it on his "holy hill," on Calvary. On the cross implanted in Zion's soil, Jesus ingested every drop of just wrath the High King of heaven had for all of our fist-shaking defiance. And why would he do that? Because the King had a gift for the Son: us. The nations who once raged at him have become his loving Bride. We are the Father's wedding gift to the Son, and he's thrilled to receive it.

At the end of this Psalm we are encouraged to "Kiss the Son." Why would we do that? Of course, we might think that this kind of kiss is just a show of feigned worship, like kissing some monarch's ring to curry his favor. But no, in this case we "worship Christ as God with the greatest reverence . . . subject [ourselves] to Christ the Lord with the greatest humility; and cling to Christ, the Bridegroom, with the greatest love."* Why do we kiss him? Because he's kissed us. Or as John

---

* Martin Luther, *Luther's Works, Vol. 14: Selected Psalms III*, ed. Jaroslav Jan Pelikan, Hilton C. Oswald, and Helmut T. Lehmann, vol. 14 (Saint Louis, MO: Concordia Publishing House, 1999), 347.

writes, "We love because he first loved us" (1 John 4:19). The Son knows very well how to quiet all our squirming and transform us into joyful daughters and sons who love to follow his lead, and that love flows down to us all the way from Zion's holy hill. You can kiss the Son today in your gracious prayer and thanksgiving and know that he delights in you.

DAY 5

I WILL NOT DIE, BUT I WILL LIVE

By Donavon Riley

I shall not die, but I shall live, and recount the deeds of the Lord.
—Psalm 118:17

It is inevitable. Whether we hold a newborn baby, narrowly avoid a car accident, or watch a segment about displaced people on the evening news, our limitations are always in front of us. Our humanness always touches us in ways that hem us in and point out our vulnerability. Even Christians are not invulnerable to the dangers that surround and impinge on us at every turn. How many of our prayers, for example, are a plea to be rescued by God from danger, especially from suffering and death?

Facing up to suffering and death, seeing it eye to eye, is not pleasurable for us. And their power to trouble and terrify us is made even more distressing by the fact that they are always accompanied by the Law and sin. In fact, whether we are worrying about a newborn, pull over to catch our breath, or turn off the television to avoid reminders of our finitude, sin and the Law always threaten us with death, especially when we wrestle and fight against them.

So long as we breathe, we are under attack from sin and death. But worse than suffering for our own sake or for the sake of a loved one, sin and death attack our faith, hope, and love toward God. Our limitations are already difficult enough to accept, but add to that the constant dread that God will not hear our prayers and rescue us and it is not a surprise when a Christian brother or sister struggles with doubt, fear, and hopelessness. A person could muster the largest military force the world has ever witnessed and it still could not do as much damage to us as when suffering and death attack our faith, hope, and love toward God.

What is even worse is that sin, the world, and Satan take what we consider the very best aspects of ourselves and use them to prove how worthless and unimportant we are, so much so that if sin does not terrify us by shoving suffering and death in our face, the best parts of ourselves are used to judge, condemn, and damn us. No matter how good we imagine ourselves to be, or how good our works are for others, there is always someone quick to point out our flaws, that one person who takes pleasure in driving us to think it would have been better had we not even bothered to try to be a good friend, spouse, child, and so on. In this way, we do not recognize the good we do as a gift from our heavenly Father but as another reminder that our limits doom us to a life of fruitless efforts at believing in God, hoping for comfort, and enjoying limitless, measureless, boundless divine love.

But no matter how it happens to us or how often sin and death are shoved in our faces, Christians must wrestle with sin and fight with death, whether in our own bodily weaknesses or as a consequence of loving others. In those times there is nothing better and more vital to us than not paying attention to ourselves or the people around us. Instead, we look away from ourselves, the world, and Satan to Christ Jesus, the Resurrection and the Life.

In relation to Jesus, we can confess that we are of no account. There is nothing remarkable or unique about us. Each of us struggles and wrestles and fights against ourselves, the world, and the devil. Each of us is flawed and fails daily to be the person we or other people want us to be. However, instead of making us even more hopeless, when we are facing the cross, staring at the Lamb of God crucified for the sin of the world, we see the final resting place of our sin and death. Everything is stripped away from us and nailed to Calvary's cross.

Jesus becomes for us our sin and death. He takes on our suffering and struggles so that in Christ by faith we can confess: "It is no longer I who struggles with sin and death but Christ in me who bears it all for me so that the life I now live, I live by faith in the One who faces off with it all for me."

Our strength to resist, wrestle, and fight against sin and death is not our own. Likewise, our good works, our holiness, our all is from God. The Lord provides our good works to us. He is our holiness because Jesus is all in all for us. We do not have to try to squeeze blood from a turnip, as the old saying goes, because we are covered and bathed by the blood of Jesus, which is a never-ending flood of grace, mercy, and truth, which is just to say, "Jesus is our life." That is why, no matter what comes against us, even when death screams in our face and terrifies us, we will not be moved because we know of absolutely nothing except God's own power that is at work in us—Jesus Christ.

DAY 6

GOD'S ENEMIES?

By Erick Sorensen

Oh that you would slay the wicked, O God! O men of blood, depart from me! They speak against you with malicious intent; your enemies take your name in vain. Do I not hate those who hate you, O Lord? And do I not loathe those who rise up against you? I hate them with complete hatred; I count them my enemies.
—Psalm 139:19-22

Not surprisingly, I haven't seen a lot of stitch art or heard a lot of praise tunes put to the warm and fuzzy words of our text. Verses 19-22 of our Psalm speaks of God's knowledge leading to condemnation of "the wicked" and "men of blood." They are described as those who are God's "enemies."

At first reading, we can easily place ourselves outside of this camp, happily throwing stones at "those bad guys over there"! But look a little closer and remember that the Bible declares in Romans 3, "None is righteous, no, not one; no one understands; no one seeks for God. All have turned aside; together they have become worthless; no one does good, not even one." We all are "quick to shed blood." By the time we get to Romans 5, what are all of us humans labeled? "Enemies" (Romans 5:8).

Now you say, "How can this be? I've never shed blood. I try to be a good person. I pay my taxes. I help out those in need sometimes. I'm not as bad as that guy across the street. (After all, he doesn't even keep up his lawn!)"

Ah, but remember, God sees our hearts. What's always been strange to me is that I often hear people refer to this as a comforting thing. Quoting God commending David for being a man after his own heart (1 Sam. 13:14), folks will seek to justify themselves by this statement. This is crazy talk . . .

Are our hearts really reflective of God's heart naturally? Not at all. Jeremiah declares, "The heart is deceitful and wicked above all things." That's the killer for us. We can probably play up a good game with our actions, looking religious and all. We can probably talk the talk. But He knows when we don't really want to do good from our hearts. He knows when we lie to ourselves from our hearts. He knows when our praise is just mouthed words, empty of meaning to us. He sees it all, and that's when we realize his judgment of us is true and right.

The Bible says we are to love God with all our hearts and all our souls and all our minds and all our strength, but we don't come anywhere close in our hearts and minds. We're divided and often lazy. Even the best of us have this wickedness within that doesn't go away.

Chuck Colson in his book *Being the Body?* tells of an interview he saw with Mike Wallace and a concentration camp survivor from World War II named Yehiel Dinur. Dinur testified against Adolf Eichmann at the Nuremberg Trials. Eighteen years before, Eichmann had sent Dinur away to Auschwitz to be gassed. This is what happened when Dinur came face-to-face in the courtroom with Eichmann:

> **Dinur began to sob uncontrollably, then fainted, collapsing in a heap on the floor as the presiding judicial officer pounded his gavel for order in the crowded courtroom. Was Dinur overcome by hatred? Fear? Horrid memories? No; it was none of these. Rather, as Dinur explained to Wallace, all at once, he realized Eichmann was not the godlike army officer who had sent so many to their**

> **deaths. This Eichmann was an ordinary man. "I was afraid of myself," said Dinur. ". . . I saw that I am capable of doing this. I am . . . exactly like him."***

Second Chronicles 16:9 says, "For the eyes of the LORD run to and fro throughout the whole earth, to give strong support to those whose heart is blameless toward him." But no one's heart is blameless toward him. The Psalms say only the truly pure in heart can ascend the holy hill of God's presence (Psalm 24:3). No one is pure, but everyone's stained with sin. So who can ascend his holy hill? Who is blameless enough to be supported? Who is perfect?

Turns out, there is only One who can pass the high bar of God's judgment, and it ain't you or me. It is only Jesus. That is why it is so essential that people place their trust in him. No one is righteous enough in and of themselves. Jesus is the only One of whom the Father says, "This is my Son, with whom I am well pleased." That is, he truly satisfies perfect justice! He has ascended God's holy hill and been found worthy. And the good news is, he brings you with him in his train just because he loves you!

As Ephesians 2 says,

> **God, being rich in mercy, because of the great love with which he loved [you], even when [you] were dead in your trespasses, made [you] alive together with Christ—by grace [you] have been saved—and raised [you] up with him and seated you with him in the heavenly places in Christ Jesus, so that in the coming ages he might show the immeasurable riches of his grace in kindness toward [you] in Christ Jesus (Ephesians 2:4-7).**

Since God knows everything, not only did He see everything we would do, but he also saw and knew what he would have to do to save us. And the good news for you is he has!

---

* Colson, Charles & Vaughn, Ellen. *Being the Body*. Nashville: Thomas Nelson, 2003. Pg. 205-206.

DAY 7

OUR HEARTS BEFORE GOD'S THRONE

By Jessica Thompson

---

*Not to us, O LORD, not to us, but to your name give glory,
for the sake of your steadfast love and your faithfulness!*
—Psalm 115:1

---

*Let no opinion of our own merits have any
room in our prayers or in our praises,
but let both center in God's glory.*
—Martin Luther*

A heart free of competition—that's what I desire. A heart that doesn't weigh my own goodness in the balances before I go to the Lord in prayer. A heart that doesn't rehearse all of my own badness before I decide I am too dirty to enter into the presence of a holy God. A heart that is done with my own glory, my own record, my own reputation. A heart that is so taken and captivated by Jesus that everything else is just a faint shadow.

---

* *Matthew Henry's Commentary on the Whole Bible: Complete and Unabridged in One Volume* (Peabody: Hendrickson, 1994).

Most days my heart is a mixture of wanting what I described above and then glory grabbing for myself. I want to prove that I am worth the glory, so I set out to be the best I can be, but inevitably I crash and fail, and once again my thoughts are on my record even though it is one of failure. The only thought that clears the clouds is to remember that God sees my fickleness, and his steadfast love and faithfulness do not diminish because of it. We never go to God on the basis of our own good works, and we should never stay away on the basis of our bad works.

The throne of grace is always available to us. For the Christian, it isn't and never will be a throne of judgment. All of the judgment for all of our sin was laid upon our perfect Savior. We are completely exposed and completely loved by God. This love doesn't waver on the days when we do bad, and it doesn't grow on the days we do good. We are loved steadfastly because of what Christ has done for us. He forever won our right standing before God by living the life we were commanded to live and dying the death that was due to us because of all of our glory grabbing. For all the times we tried to glory grab, we are covered by Christ's perfect record of humility and we are forgiven and cleansed by his precious blood. God's faithfulness will never end.

So with confidence, dear sisters, with confidence draw near to him—confidence in his work, confidence in his love. You will not find a smack and a disappointed head shake. Rest assured that you will find mercy and grace to help with your day there. You will find a Savior who sympathizes with you in your weaknesses, a Father who delights in you. Draw near. Draw near with haste.

Let us then with confidence draw near to the throne of grace, that we may receive mercy and find grace to help in time of need.
—Hebrews 4:16

DAY 8

SALVATION BELONGS TO THE LORD

By Joel Fitzpatrick

O LORD, how many are my foes! Many are rising against me; many are saying of my soul, "There is no salvation for him in God." Selah. But you, O LORD, are a shield about me, my glory, and the lifter of my head. I cried aloud to the Lord, and he answered me from his holy hill. Selah. I lay down and slept; I woke again, for the Lord sustained me. I will not be afraid of many thousands of people who have set themselves against me all around. Arise, O LORD! Save me, O my God. For you strike all my enemies on the cheek; you break the teeth of the wicked. Salvation belongs to the LORD; your blessing be on your people!
—Psalm 3

The King is on his throne ruling! Hooray! This was the news Israel was waiting for, and now it had happened. Psalm 1 and 2 declare the glory of the reign of David, and they point us forward to the coming rule and reign of Christ and all is well, right? Not really.

It can be easy to think that the Christian life will be one successive victory after another, and frankly, that is the tone that we would expect the Psalms to take after the announcement of the King. But the Psalms do anything but present a sugar-coated presentation of the Christian life. In fact, they are decidedly real about the missed expectations we face so often.

Unfulfilled dreams, lost status, the threat of enemies from outside, and the voice of the enemy within—this is where we find King David and his son Absalom threatening to kill him and to take the kingdom from him, a massive betrayal. In the face of this betrayal, he cries this lament out to God.

David starts with, "O Lord!" He calls on the covenant name of God. He reminds God that he is the covenant-keeping God that put David on the throne, and he says, "Look, all around me are my enemies! They are everywhere. They are attacking me physically and spiritually. I am desperate. I don't see any escape." I wonder if you know what it is to be David at this point. It may be from physical enemies, broken friendships, cancer, or divorce. It may be Satan, the age-old enemy accusing you at every step. You are exhausted and feeling hopeless, yet you still know what is supposed to be true about God.

David is afraid, in a dark, scary place. Here we read these beautiful words, these words of hope and life: "But you, Lord." Notice the great reversal of fortunes, even in the middle of the same circumstances. David has enemies all around him, pressing in on him, calling into question God's love and care for him, the king. He turns from this state of confusion to remembering God, and that brings him back to a place where he rests in the work of the covenant-keeping God on his behalf. David goes from someone who had enemies all around him, feeling the oppression of his enemies and the questioning of his beliefs to a man who is rooted and grounded in his covenant-keeping God.

David calls out to the heavens, and God answers. C.S. Lewis in his book *Surprised by Joy* talks about praying and having the feeling that the doors to heaven are closed and are made of brass, so often this can be our experience. This is really frustrating, and we wonder where God is. This Psalm assures us of two things: first, God is on his holy hill. He is in heaven, where he hears us. Second, God answers us from this holy place of power.

This brings the king to the point where he is able to escape sleepless nights, full of hope and rest instead of fear. Look at the way verses 4-6 start (notice the progression): I cried; I lay down; I woke again; I will not be afraid. These four staccato verbs present four ordinary actions that come from one extraordinary God. When I am in the middle of the strife, when I am in the midst of suffering, and when I have come to the end of myself, the only thing I want to be able to do is to sleep. Recently, my wife miscarried. It was devastating. When we thought that we had finally made it through the worst of the mourning, we were plunged back in again. I found out that I was losing my job. All I wanted was to sleep. I felt like we would never get out of it. I longed to feel the trust in God that David did.

David turns to God in verse 7 and speaks to him with confidence: "Arise! Save me!" What we don't notice as we read this in English is that these verbs are imperatives. This gives the impression that David is commanding God to do something. He is calling on God to show himself to be what he is, a "shield about me, my glory, and the lifter of my head" (v. 3).

How can we have this confidence? How can we know that even though we were God's enemies, even though we were and still act like the wicked, that God will not break our teeth? It is because Jesus was struck, and struck, and struck again to the point where he was unrecognizable. He had his flesh ripped from his bones. He had his teeth broken as if he was one of the wicked. He was nailed to the cross, died, and was buried. He had enemies all around him, and yet he prayed, "Father . . . not my will, but yours, be done" (Luke 22:42). Jesus placed his confidence in his Father, the covenant-keeping God, and even when it seemed that the heavens turned to brass for him when the Father poured out his unmitigated wrath, Jesus never faltered. He had his head laid in a grave, and three days later, he awoke by the power of the Spirit as the conqueror.

He did all of this so that when we fail, when our faith falters, Jesus's perfect record stands in our broken place. So now we can sleep and awake, knowing that this same covenant-keeping God is our God. This thought should so fill your heart with joy that you can cry out just like David did, "Salvation belongs to the Lord; your blessing be on your people!" (v. 8).

DAY 9

HUNTED BY GOODNESS AND MERCY

By Daniel Emery Price

There is no psalm as well known as Psalm 23. Sometimes when a portion of scripture is this well known, it becomes a sort of cliché or platitude. You also see this with John 3:16, Romans 8:28, and many others. But these texts are well known for a reason. They contain comforts and promises that Christians have clung to from the time of the early church.

I have read the well-worn verses of the twenty-third Psalm countless times, but as I read them again recently, I was surprised at how the comforting words of David hit me as if I had never read them before.

- The Lord is our Shepherd who brings us to his soul-restoring water.
- He walks with us through the desperate valley of the shadow of death.
- He comforts us with the rod of his cross, and he uses it to defeat death.
- He faithfully guides us with the staff of his word to his gift-laden table.
- He serves us himself in the presence of our enemies: sin, death, and the devil.

Every line is rich with wonderful, peace-giving words of comfort, hope, and promise. Psalm 23 is only six verses long, but in that sixth and final verse, David says something utterly incredible—and it's easily missed.

Surely goodness and mercy shall follow me all the days of my life, and I shall dwell in the house of the Lord forever.
—Psalm 23:6

Follow is not a word we struggle to understand. It's a word we use all the time. If I'm going somewhere with a group of people and I don't know the way, I will say to someone else who does, "I'll follow you." And in the context of Psalm 23, I think we all assume "goodness and mercy" following us means something like "they will always be around" or "we're never far from them." But that's not really what the text is saying.

The word we translate as *follow* is the Hebrew word *radap*. It means: "to pursue or chase down." In other words, God's goodness and mercy are not passively hanging around behind us. They are actively pursuing us. They are chasing us down. Like a lion hunting its prey, so the goodness and mercy of God are hounding us. God is the Hunter, and he has given chase. There is no escape. We will find ourselves caught time and time again by a good and merciful God.

We know David had days of incredible victory and days of incredible defeat—days of humbling obedience and days of impassioned sin. He had days of meditation on the word of God and days of running, wondering, and even brazen unrepentance. But he makes no distinction between any of these days when speaking of this relentless goodness and mercy of God. Their unstoppable hounding has been the constant through "all the days" of his life. And so it is with us.

Psalm 23 tells us we have nothing to fear. Even when we find ourselves in the valley of the shadow of death, our great Good Shepherd goes with us. And those rapidly approaching footsteps you hear are not those of the devil coming to do you in—they belong to the Holy Hunter, and they are known as the goodness and mercy of God.

DAY 10

THE TRUE MAN

By Jared C. Wilson

---

*Therefore the wicked will not stand in the judgment, nor sinners in the congregation of the righteous; for the L*ORD *knows the way of the righteous, but the way of the wicked will perish.*
—Psalm 1:5-6

You and I are starving for the glory of God. Underneath all the desires, all the longings, all the cravings, and all the yearnings, this is our fundamental and essential need—an experience of the magnitude and the character of the God of the universe.

Psalm 1:5-6 speaks to this need as the spiritual diagnosis of all that plagues us. All of our not fitting in, all of our anxiety, all of our brokenness rests on top of the primary problem of our not being able "to stand." God is holy, and we are not. Thus everything wrong flows from this essential wrongness. Because if *standing* in the judgment (v. 5) means, in part, not walking in the counsel of the wicked or standing in the way of sinners or sitting in the seat of scoffers, as the psalmist says back in verse 1, I'm in deep trouble. And I assume you are too.

The situation could not be more bleak. The echo of the law of righteousness reverberates so loudly and powerfully in these two verses, that not a single one of us can help from being blown over by its force. The law is the great equalizer. It puts every one of us on the same level, and it levels every one of us.

What are we to do?

Interestingly enough, the emphasis of the entirety of Psalm 1, actually, is not much on things to do. Oh yes, there are certainly things to do. The law is good at telling us good things to do, things that accord with "the way of the righteous." And yet, we notice that the tone of Psalm 1 isn't primarily about things to do but rather experiencing things that are *done*—more specifically, things that are done *for us*.

Here is the staggering and perplexing beauty of the gospel. The solution to our inscrutable problem of our doing wrong things is not fundamentally our doing right things but having the right things done on our behalf. This is why, for instance, the psalm reads so much in the passive voice.

Apart from the sovereign intervention of the Lord, we would be utterly and hopelessly lost. But by his grace, we "are planted," as the psalmist says in verse 1.

And this is why I love Psalm 1:6: "For the LORD knows the way of the righteous." It speaks not immediately to a right religion but to a right relationship. To know of God is vitally important, and to know about God is crucial to righteous living, but to be known by God trumps it all. There is nothing more precious than to be known by God, to be reconciled to him by the atoning work of his Son Jesus Christ, who by his blood has made us sons and daughters along with him.

The tone of Psalm 1 is not on things to do but on things that are. Because of this, we are left to conclude that the person Psalm 1 is describing has not necessarily achieved the blessings of verse 1 by doing and not doing all that's discussed, but that the person is doing and not doing all that's discussed because of the blessing of verse 1.

In other words, we don't do stuff to get this blessing. We get this blessing, and then we do stuff. The tree imagery in verse 3 certainly speaks to this. Having been planted by streams of water, the tree almost cannot help flourishing in leaves and fruit.

We do receive blessings from our faith and works, but faith and works are received from an original blessing. The man who does not walk in the way of sin understands he is blessed.

Psalm 1 describes the kind of man who seems, by most indications, to be perfect. Meditates on the law day and night? Do *you* do that? Well, maybe it just means "throughout the day and night," at regular intervals. Do you do that? I don't. It would seem in fact that Psalm 1 is describing perfect personhood, establishing a description of the soul submitted to heaven, the aspiration and ambition of all the psalms that come after it. Psalm 1 is the gory cross-section of a "true person." And since we who are sinners saved by grace know that we are in the flesh fundamentally *dis*ordered persons, we can see that Psalm 1 is actually a better description of the one true man, the second Adam without sin, Jesus Christ.

Jesus is the man who walks not in the counsel of the wicked but in perfect submission to the Father. Jesus is the man who does not stand in the way of sinners but is the friend of sinners, becoming the very way himself that they find salvation. Jesus is the man who does not sit in the seat of scoffers but in the seat of mercy. Jesus is the man whose delight is in the law of the Lord, and he always lives to intercede for his siblings. Jesus is the man who on the law meditates day and night, for he does not sleep or slumber, and his holiness is everlasting.

Jesus is like a tree—the tree of life planted by streams of water, living water that, whoever drinks of it will never be thirsty again, water that yields its fruit in its season, the fruit of the Spirit, *against which there is no law*, and its leaf does not wither, but is instead the true vine, in whom we abide as branches.

In all that he does, Jesus prospers. He never fails. The wicked are not so, of course, but are like chaff that the wind drives away. But he commands the wind. He is the rock, the firm foundation, the cornerstone, the withstander and the driver of every storm. The wicked will not stand in the judgment, nor sinners in the congregation of the righteous, but he will be the judge himself, and despite standing in the judgment of the cross, he will be not ashamed to call redeemed sinners his brothers.

The Lord knows the way of the righteous, because he is the way of the righteous.

DAY 11

ASKING AND THANKING

By Steven Paulson

You have to deal with God one way or another, as David says: "When you hide your face, they are dismayed; when you take away their breath, they die and return to their dust. When you send forth your Spirit, they are created, and you renew the face of the ground" (Psalm 104:29-30).

How much better to have God sent in Spirit—that means with a preacher, rather than hiding without one!

Before the preacher arrives, people are living (often rather well), but they must make a deal with the devil like Goethe's Faust taking some stance toward death. They usually just deny death, but if they still have some energy that attempts to be courageous, grasping their fate (Nietzsche). Live every day as if it were your last! But Christians cannot deny death because of the crucifixion of Christ. If it happened to him, it will happen to us—but there is a cure. Once a preacher comes, we learn to fear God and just so lose our fear of death.

Those who fear God say, "Manifold are your works!" (Psalm 104:24).

Not my works but God's will provides everything necessary for life. God's works are his words he speaks to you by a preacher in which he gives two great gifts of prayer.

The first is to know whom to *thank* for your bounty. Most do not know this. When I eat with pagans, they awkwardly pause, wondering if there should be a prayer because a preacher is in their midst. I take pity on them since they do not know the most basic matter of life. So I say, "Let's thank our Lord and Savior Jesus Christ, who has given us everything needed for life!"

If you do not have the right God to thank for this good, the responsibility for securing your goods falls back upon yourself. When an uncle sends a check, a niece should write a letter of thanks. Yet the problem is not just that people should learn how to say thank you as a courtesy but that when you don't know whom to thank, you start thanking yourself. Praise turns inward. This is a double bondage. When you have only yourself to thank, you end up having only yourself to depend upon. I have a family member who prays: "Thank you, Universe." Now, in part, this is just to stick it to the Christians, but mainly it is to ignore both her maker and the many people sitting around the table who have sacrificed as means for God to give things to her. Instead, she composes a dream that "the universe will provide"—until it does not.

Here the second gift is even greater: to know whom to *ask* when you are in need. Only faith knows where to go in times of trouble. Believing that God is my creator is no piece of cake since what I need is sometimes taken from me precisely because faith is in that which is not seen. Then the hardest part of praying is learning to pray against my own feelings.

So David teaches us how to pray: "These all look to you, to give them their food in due season" (Psalm 104:27).

Who are we waiting for? The Lord, the Giver of life! Otherwise, people do not know who feeds them and end up like New Yorkers who have never seen a farmer. For this reason, J. S. Bach used this Psalm at the beginning of Cantata 187. The choir begins with the hymn: "All things wait upon Thee that thou mayest give them their meat in due season."

The reason we should pray comes after the bass aria sings Matthew 6: "Take no thought saying, 'What shall we eat or what shall we drink . . . for your heavenly father knows they you have need of all these things.'"

Then the soprano sings: "God provides all life that breathes on this earth. Is He to deny me alone that which He promises to all others? Begone worries! His pledge also embraces me and is renewed daily to me by many acts of fatherly love."

It is always a great occasion to assemble your family or even when eating alone, to pray this way. Then you are freed from the fear of death and learn to speak to a loving Father: "My Lord, look at how you take care of me, even when I do nothing or even worse, offend you. You give me food, clothing, home, family, etc., though I do not deserve it."

DAY 12

DON'T IGNORE THE WORM

By Cindy Koch

But I am a worm and not a man, scorned by mankind and despised by the people.
—Psalm 22:6

Small, disgraceful maggot. Chewing on the left-over garbage. Squirming in the mud, beneath the feet of people above. He writhes, and they shudder. He drags across the ground, and they gag. There is no honor in the disgusting path of a worm.

Yet here he stands, the maggot of a man. Forgotten by other people, depressed by his insignificant life. Hated by the beautiful, condemned by the popular. Broken by those who should have loved. Weary of the constant pain. Shamed for the things he has done. Tormented by the times he didn't help. Sickened by his own self. He's a weak and helpless worm left to die.

Yes, I know. You want to turn away from this tiny maggot of filth. We would all rather focus our attention on more grand and beautiful things. Maybe you could turn this page to a more hopeful psalm, one that triumphs over the sadness—words of praise and thanksgiving for the wonderful salvation of God. It is a psalm that shouts and sings the glories of the almighty Lord! But not this. Not a slimy, dirty worm wallowing in the dust.

Even he admits this with you, my friend. The worm of a man screams at his God, "You are holy, oh my God. You have a high and mighty home upon the praises of Israel! You are wonderful, my God. You are glorious, my Lord. My fathers trusted you, and they were delivered. Your chosen people for generations have called to you, and they were rescued from this shame. You, oh my God, have done grand and beautiful and hopeful things for those others. But me? Here I am, scraping the ground with my naked belly. I am a pitiful worm, ashamed."

The overwhelming realization of our stature before our holy God leaves you sick. Nothing you have to give makes you worthy of God's love. Nothing you have done has earned an ounce of praise from our holy Lord. Instead, here you discover that you mindlessly destroy yourself and others in this cycle of sin in which you are imprisoned. It would be the more pleasant devotion to ignore the worm in this psalm. It would be the more comfortable thing to ignore the worm within you.

> **But she came and knelt before him, saying, "Lord, help me." And (Jesus) answered, "It is not right to take the children's bread and throw it to the dogs." She said, "Yes, Lord, yet even the dogs eat the crumbs that fall from their masters' table." (Matthew 15:25-27)**

She also comes to the Lord, crying, squirming, dirty, and unclean—so far from any worth, she can claim for her own. This outcast Samaritan woman crawls up to the wonderous promised Messiah and admits boldly who she is. Yes, Lord, I am a dog. I do not deserve your gifts or your mercy. Yes, my God, I am a worm. Help me.

And Jesus, walking and breathing flesh of man, Word of God begotten of the Father, does exactly that. He helps her. He becomes the dog that she is. Jesus, sinless human, Son of God, does it all. He helps the man in the psalm. He becomes the worm that men despise. Jesus, born of a woman, Savior of the world, does the thing you cannot. He helps you.

> **And about the ninth hour Jesus cried out with a loud voice, saying, "Eli, Eli, lema sabachthani?" that is, "My God, my God, why have you forsaken me?" And Jesus cried out again with a loud voice and yielded up his spirit. (Matthew 27:46, 50)**

"My God, My God, why have you forsaken me?" The worm screams from the cross for every distant or wicked word you have ever muttered with your tongue or in your heart. "Why are you so far from saving me?" The maggot shrieks as the black chains of your sin suffocate his every breath for every misdirected thought and desire that ever passed through your mind. But it is here he helps you. He is the dog. He is the worm. He, instead, is the despised and condemned man—the worm who you used to be.

Jesus throws himself perfectly upon the mercy of God. Abandoning every glorious effort of his own, he completely repents for you, completely trusts for you, completely fulfills the penalty of death for you. Wholly God, his payment is acceptable to the divine judge. Wholly man, his death is properly substitutionary for this flesh and blood creation. The only begotten worm of a man is raised from the grave to reign at the right hand of God. And it is here he helps even you. His new life is yours.

So don't ignore the worm. It is by his death and resurrection that you receive life. Boldly we crawl, blessed worms, unafraid of those who threaten from above. We wriggle in the mud, as forgiven maggots, feeding only on his heavenly food from above, disgusting and rotten among ourselves, but pure and perfect by the blood of Jesus. As worms, we daily cry out, "Help us, Lord, my God." And in Christ, he already has.

DAY 13

ILL-CONCEIVED: PINPOINTING WHEN OUR LIVES WENT WRONG

By Chad Bird

The little psychologist within us is often hard at work to pinpoint the origin of life's problems. During marital strife, we sift through everything from sexual proclivities to spending habits to discover the source of our discontent. When raising a rebellious child, we replay every episode in his upbringing to determine where things may have gone awry. We want to know when Pandora's box was cracked open and mayhem invaded our lives.

The answer to this question is hidden in the heart of Psalm 51.

The poet laments his wrongdoing: "I know my transgressions, and my sin is always before me. . . . Against you, you only, have I sinned, and done what is evil in your sight" (Psalm 51:3–4). He describes himself as unclean. God needs to wash him, to blot out his sins. The Lord has broken his bones, and he fears the loss of the Holy Spirit.

Why did David sin so grievously? Was it his kingship that engendered an I-can-have-anyone-I-want attitude? Was it his lust-filled heart that enticed him to bed Bathsheba and kill her husband?

Perhaps all of these had a part to play, but he highlights none of these. In fact, he takes us back to much earlier in his life, to the deepest, earliest source of his sins.

He says, "Behold, I was brought forth in iniquity, and in sin did my mother conceive me" (v. 5). Not when he was a king crowned, but when he was a baby conceived, things went wrong with David.

And with all of us. We do not begin our existence as humans with a clean slate. We are conceived as fully flawed people, heirs of corruption. As Moses wrote, "Every intention of the thoughts of his heart was only evil continually" (Genesis 6:5). Only. Evil. Continually. That sad triad of words would serve well as the title of the biography of humanity.

What is it about David's life, and this psalm, that make this so fitting a place to utter this dire pronouncement of humanity's corruption?

David gives perfect expression to the imperfection that has poisoned our very nature. He lacked for nothing, yet wanted more. As Nathan would chide him:

> **Thus says the Lord, the God of Israel, "I anointed you king over Israel, and I delivered you out of the hand of Saul. And I gave you your master's house and your master's wives into your arms and gave you the house of Israel and of Judah. And if this were too little, I would add to you as much more. Why have you despised the word of the Lord, to do what is evil in his sight?" (2 Samuel 12:7-9)**

Notice the God-verbs: I anointed, I delivered, I gave, I would have added. It's like the garden of Eden all over again. On this Adam-like David, God piled gift upon gift upon gift. Yet still that forbidden, female fruit David plucked. Curved in on himself, David craved what the Lord had not given to satisfy his own lust and greed and selfishness.

I have done that too. And you have as well. Why? The sin in which our mothers conceived us conceives in us all manner of evil.

What is rather startling, however, is that hidden within this verse is the story of another David whose birth, indeed, whose conception, changes everything. If not a single cell of sanctity is ours, if not a vestige of original purity is tucked away in the folds of our being, then the only way in which we have hope must be found in someone outside ourselves. If our conception is sinful, we need one whose conception was pure for us. If our birth is in iniquity, we need one whose birth was holy for us. If our lives constantly ooze selfishness and greed and lust, then we need one whose life was replete with righteousness, who resisted every temptation, who kept every divine law flawlessly for us.

That is why the Son of God did not appear on earth as a full-grown man. He came into this world via the womb, as we all do. He passed through every stage of life that we pass through, but he did so perfectly, that in his perfection, we might receive our own perfection in the eyes of the Father. For Christ was not conceived for himself, but for us. He was not born for himself, but for us. He did not keep God's commandments for himself, but for us. He did not die and rise again for himself, but yes, for us. He fully meant what he said when he told his disciples, "I did not come to be served, but to serve." The service of Jesus for us began in utero, for in utero our service to self began.

Psalm 51 is ultimately much more than the prayer of David's repentance, as well as ours. It is the proclamation of the gospel of a new and better David, whose conception conceives within us new hope of a new life of forgiveness and reconciliation to the Father. This David, this Jesus, blots out our transgressions, washes us thoroughly from iniquities, and cleanses us from our sins. For from conception to cross, from full womb to empty tomb, he is the sole source and cause of our salvation.

DAY 14

WILL GOD FORGIVE ME . . . AGAIN?

By Bruce Hillman

Blessed is the one whose transgression is forgiven, whose sin is covered. Blessed is the man against whom the LORD counts no iniquity, and in whose spirit there is no deceit.
—Psalm 32:1-2

There is a man I know who fought in the Vietnam War. I have tried to get him to come to church many times, but each time he refuses because he says that his crimes are so great that God could not forgive him. Though I press him with the good news of the gospel that covers over all his sins, he refuses to believe that his record of wrongdoing can be erased by merely believing in Christ.

What my friend finds difficult to accept is a notion the psalmist wants to teach us. There is a way of thinking about a person who receives forgiveness, namely, that such a person is *blessed*. We do well to ask what it means to be blessed. Simply, to be blessed is to be *favored*.

Sometimes when our guilt sticks heavily upon us, we can wonder if God's forgiveness really applies to us. We do that certain sin, again and again, we surprise ourselves with some out-of-character action, we find ourselves feeling less guilty for certain trespasses, etc. In the midst of such rhythms, we are to take the psalmist's prayer to heart. For we are reminded here that we are favored by God. God has taken our sins away *because God wants to!*

It is hard to believe this because there seems an inherent injustice in it. "If I keep sinning and doing bad, won't God punish me? Isn't his job to keep order? I know he is patient, but I keep repeating the same mistakes. At some point God is going to drop the hammer on me, isn't he?"

This sense of dreadful anticipation at God's coming wrath is real because guilty people know that justice must eventually come. God can't keep turning a blind eye. And he doesn't. We must put away a whitewashed Christianity that says that God simply forgives because He is nice, kind, loving, gentle, etc. That is not how forgiveness works. God does not simply ignore our sins, turn a blind eye to them, and perpetuate injustice. No. God has forgiven you *for Christ's sake*. It was because Jesus paid your debt, took your penalty, and ransomed you from sin and death that you are forgiven. St. Paul has a special word to describe the new, objective reality of your forgiveness: *justification*. Notice the word "justice" embedded within it. Justification is God's work, at Christ's expense, to free you from sin, death, and hell. It is justice done to sin and grace given to you. *And God wanted to do this for you.*

When God forgives you for the sins you commit over and over, he does so because Christ has paid for their trespass and received the justice of the crime. God does not turn a blind eye to sin but instead issues justice upon his Son, for your sake.

This means you are blessed or favored because God loves you enough, because Jesus loves you enough, to hold no record of your wrongs. Now, if we are so favored by God that he would not spare his only Son, how much more so will he then help us in the midst of our troubles? You see, the cross teaches us the dedication to which God will go to show his favor for you. He wants to forgive you! So now, as you struggle through various trials, do not be downtrodden. The God who never abandoned you to your own sin will not abandon you now. And though you sin ten times ten thousand times, you can never out-sin the work of the cross. Let us live in this promise.

DAY 15

TINY, WEAK, AND CARED FOR

By Elyse Fitzpatrick

When I look at the heavens, the work of your fingers, the moon and the stars, which you have set in place, what is man that you are mindful of him, and the son of man that you care for him?
—*Psalm 8:3-4*

Okay, I have a confession to make: I'm kind of an astronomy nerd. I love looking at pictures from the Hubble telescope. In fact, one time I took my grandson up to the Jet Propulsion Laboratory in Pasadena, to see life-size models of the Voyager and the room where they built it. I've toured the Palomar Observatory and joined in nighttime stargazing parties in Sequoia National Park. And I also tune in every time SpaceX is scheduled to fire a rocket. I love the heavens. They shock and amaze me, and I admit that sometimes I wish I were an astrophysicist and could really explore the way I want to. But alas, I'm old and I hate math. So when I start thinking this way, I console myself by saying that I'm sure that exploring the heavens is something I'll enjoy doing when I get to the New Earth. Will there be nebulas there? I hope so.

Perhaps one reason I find the heavens so fascinating is that I know and love their Creator: "In the beginning, God created the heavens"

(Genesis 1:1). I love those words and am amazed at God's power. All humankind combining all their power couldn't make one nebula. Not even one. But here's how David described their creation: he called them the work of the Lord's "fingers." Get that. The moon and all the stars, the galaxies and all the worlds, all nebulas and black holes, and planets that are billions of light-years from earth are all simply the work of his fingers—just a couple of swipes with his ring finger and pinky. No big thing for him. Enormous horizons of universe after universe that we could never explore even if we had a thousand lifetimes were created by him as "hand-made sky-jewelry . . . mounted in their settings."* Sky-jewelry . . . think of that! The earth is the Lord's art project. He made it the way it is because he delights in beauty and there's no end to his creativity and power.

David's words here are meant to make us feel our insignificance. We're tiny. We're weak. If his fingers created all the heavens, then in comparison to his power and enormity, we don't even amount to a grain of sand in the Sahara. And so, David voices the most logical of questions: What is man that you are mindful of him, and the son of man that you care for him (v. 4)?

To answer that question, we need to think back to the creation of the earth. On the sixth day, after he had bejeweled the heavens with stars and the earth with incalculable plants and animals, the Lord said, "Let us make man in our image, after our likeness . . . So God created man in his own image, in the image of God he created him" (Genesis 1:26-27). And "God blessed them . . . and God saw everything that he had made, and behold, it was very good" (Genesis 1:28, 31). Why is God "mindful" of us? Why does he "care" for us? Simply because man, though infinitesimal in comparison to the heavens, is his image-bearer. He made us to be particularly like him in ways that sugar cane, grizzly bears, or Neptune aren't, and because we reflect him in this way, he keeps us in mind always. Humankind is the crown of all God created. So he cares for us as we might care for a beautiful painting we created and delight in.

---

* Eugene H. Peterson, *The Message: The Bible in Contemporary Language* (Colorado Springs, CO: NavPress, 2005), Ps 8:3.

But that's not the only reason we fill his thoughts. Yes, he cares for us because we're created in his image, but he also cares for us because the second person of the Trinity, the Son, became one of us. He took to himself the blood, bone, and DNA (creations of God) of a little virgin girl, and his incarnation has forever elevated our race. Jesus is the image of the true God, but he is also the true man. By living in perfect loving obedience to his Father, Jesus truly fulfilled all that man had been created to be and has graciously credited us with that record. And because of that, when we put our trust in him, we can have complete assurance that God, who has numbered all the stars and "gives to all of them their names" (Psalm 147:4), knows our name and knows us so well that he can tell you how many hairs are on your head. "Fear not," the perfect Man says to us, "you are of more value than many sparrows" (Luke 12:7). Or stars or nebula or grizzlies. Don't be afraid. You're more than a speck of dust to him. You're his beloved. He's all-powerful and knows you intimately. And even so, he loves you. What are we that he is mindful and cares for us? His beloved.

DAY 16

YOU ARE NOT FORGOTTEN

By Donavon Riley

Out of the depths I cry to You, O Lord.
—Psalm 130:1

When the psalmist writes, "Out of the depths I cry to You, O Lord" (Psalm 130:1), what is he crying out for from the Lord? He is pleading for grace. In the most profound sense of the word, the psalmist is crying out for God to deliver grace to him in his deepest distress. And this is the rub. We, like the psalmist, only cry out for grace when we have made a mess of life, are trapped in our self-destructive habits, and feel God has forsaken us. What the psalmist writes can only be understood by people who have felt and experienced what it is like to fall headlong into horrible misery and hopelessness. Nobody thinks to pray for grace who has not first been knocked down and terrified by sin and death.

We can go days, even years, without feeling the consequences of our own selfish decisions. But when they catch up with us and their weight falls on us, overwhelming us, driving us to throw up our hands and cry out to God for rescue, then we cry out for grace. It is only when the power of sin and death push down on us, like a winepress expressing juice from grapes, that a prayer for grace in the deepest sense of the word is extracted from us. Only when we are in the worst of situations do we cry out for God to be God for us in the most unconditional sense. When we have lost all hope in ourselves or any other person, even when we lose hope that God himself will be for us, do we cry out of the depths, "Lord, have mercy on me!"

Only God can forgive our sin, rescue us from death, and create a joyful and peaceful heart in us. But we do not usually look for this, because we are obsessed with God forgiving, rescuing, and creating for us in ways we choose. We can heap sin upon sin on ourselves, and still, we will not turn to the Lord for his absolute absolution until all escapes have been closed to us. We prefer God to forgive our sin by not paying attention to it. Then our prayer is not for grace but that God would overlook and wink at us from the sidelines.

Likewise, God's judgment is for other people. Most of the time we do not fear God, and we do not even consider the very real consequences of his judgment, not toward sin, or how the condemnation intended for us is redirected onto the crucified Lamb of God. Instead, we imagine that so long as we recognize that we have done wrong in relation to God, that is enough of a confession that He will not point an accusing finger at us. That is why, unless we are overwhelmed and knocked flat on our back by sin and death, we do not fear God. We hate God and resist his grace.

That is why for the psalmist, fear and hope go hand in hand. When we fear God has forsaken us on account of our selfish, self-destructive choices, then we cry out in the hope that he will hear us and rescue us from ourselves. Then, when we cry out for grace, we are pointed to the cross. There at Golgotha, all our fears of judgment and hope for grace are laid bare. There on the cross, we are put to death. Jesus expresses our cries of dereliction. He hangs on our cross and cries out of the depths for us. When we look at the Lamb of God stretched out on Calvary's cross, we behold God's answer to our cries.

We are not forgotten. Our cries are not ignored. We are not laid flat by sin and left for dead. Our refuge in every trouble and horror and terror is nailed to the cursed tree. Therefore there is no other place for the psalmist or us to run for grace than the person of Jesus Christ. This man who is God for us is our forgiveness, life, and salvation. He is the biblical meaning of grace—not some idea in search of meaning, but the limitless, abundant, inexhaustible grace of God on two legs. And when He is for us, as the apostle writes, who can be against us? With Jesus alone is forgiveness. In relation to the Christ, and Him only, is there grace upon grace. In relation to the Lamb of God, there is only one answer to our deepest cries for grace: "I will never leave you or forsake you because I have called you by name and you are mine."

DAY 17

TASTE THE GOODNESS

By Erick Sorensen

Oh, taste and see that the Lord is good! Blessed is the man who takes refuge in him!
—Psalm 34:8

I love apologetics, the art and science of defending the Christian faith. I love talking about all the philosophical arguments for the existence of God with my skeptical friends. I love sharing the various pieces of evidence for the resurrection of Jesus Christ. I *love* the fact that Christianity does not call us to "just shut up and believe what we're told," but to trust in real eyewitness testimony that took place in a real place at a real time.

But sometimes . . .

Sometimes, no amount of evidence, argumentation, berating, or anything else will do it for us (even though there are plenty of good arguments and evidence for the Christian faith). Sometimes, there's no better response to skepticism than the words of our Psalm: "Taste and see that the Lord is good."

I basically have the palate of an eight-year-old boy who is just fine eating mac and cheese, SpaghettiOs with franks, and hamburgers every day. But living in New York has forced me to expand my palate. A little while back a friend of mine offered to buy me and a friend lunch at this really nice restaurant. But there was a catch: being aware of my little boy taste buds, my friend said, "I get to order for you, and you have to eat everything they bring out." I was extremely cautious, but hey, it was a free lunch, so I agreed to his dictum. Soon, things were being brought out to our table that I never dreamed of trying, scary-looking things whose name I still don't know.

At that moment, no amount of reason would have gotten my picky eight-year-old palate to eat any of those things. No matter how much they told me it was delicious or that it was good for me, I wouldn't have believed them. I just had to taste and see. I had to experience it. And you know what? Most of it was really good!

Perhaps you're reading this today struggling to see that the Lord is good. Where can you go to "taste" of his goodness again?

You're probably expecting at this point to receive a few different suggestions:

1. Spend a long time in prayer.
2. Read a bunch of scripture that deals with what to do when you're struggling.
3. Turn on some worship music and sing along loudly.

All of these things would be good, right, and almost undoubtedly edifying. But you know there is a place where you can literally "taste" and see that the Lord is good—a place where you don't have to do anything but simply receive what is given. That place is at the communion table.

There at the table, the sacrifice Christ endured for you is made visible. There at the table, you hear it declared to you again that yes, it's really true: your sins are forgiven. There at the table, you're brought into a fellowship bigger than yourself. There at the table, you get a foretaste of the feast that awaits us in heaven.

Oh, taste and see that the Lord is good! Blessed are you who takes refuge in him.

DAY 18

BECOMING LIKE WEANED CHILDREN

By Jessica Thompson

I am sure each one of us has seen a baby sitting on a mom's lap who wants to eat. The baby is rooting around looking for something, really anything to latch on to. It wants its milk, and it wants it now! There is no reasoning with a baby that is looking to nurse. You can't assure it of its mother's love and tell it that things will be okay. If that baby does not get what it wants in a timely manner, you and everyone in earshot will know the baby's complaint. I am also sure that you have seen a baby who no longer nurses sitting in the lap of its mother. It is often times just happy to be near the mom, not wanting anything but to be close. This baby has been weaned; it doesn't rely on its mother's body to produce the food that sustains it. This baby is content to lean against the mother's breasts without needing to be attached and taking from the mom.

In Psalm 131, David relates to the weaned child. "But I have calmed and quieted my soul, like a weaned child with its mother; like a weaned child is my soul within me" (v. 2) In the opening of the psalm David talks about how his "heart is not lifted up" and how his eyes "are not raised too high." He is making a confession of humble dependence on his Father. He isn't trying to understand all of life, and in fact, he sees he cannot understand all of life. He says that he does not occupy himself "with things too great and too marvelous" for him. He is placing all of his hope in the love, power, and care of his Father. He is displaying the childlike faith that Jesus commends in Matthew 18:3 when he said, "unless you turn and become like children, you will never enter the kingdom of heaven." This faith is completely stripped of its own merit. This faith reclines upon the bosom of another and trusts that all that is needed will be given. This faith is weaned from its own understanding of what needs to happen for life to be sustained, and it believes. This faith confesses the validity of Jesus's words when he tells us that we don't need to worry about tomorrow. We don't need to worry about what we will eat or what we will drink. We can with great confidence rest in the care of our heavenly Father. He knows what you need. He invites you to calm and quiet your soul.

I would like to tell you all that I have learned this discipline that I am like a weaned child living in full quietness, confident in God's love and care for me. I cannot. I oftentimes am restless and full of anxiousness, wondering what is going to happen next, wondering if God will continue to take care of me. The glorious news of the gospel is that even in my restless, anxious wondering, God looks at me and sees His Son's perfect record of saying, "Not my will but yours be done." I am no longer considered the petty, small-minded, suspicious child concerned about my next meal. I am now the Son who knew that the Father's love would sustain. I am forgiven for my lack of faith. I am forgiven for my lack of trust. I am accepted wholly in the Beloved.

It is that good news that gives me the courage to say what David says in verse 3 of this psalm, "O Israel, hope in the LORD for this time forth and forevermore." Beloved child of God, hope in the Lord. He has provided your greatest need. He has raised you from the dead and given you life. He has taken you out of the kingdom of darkness and transferred you into the kingdom of his beloved Son. He has forgiven every single one of your trespasses. He has made you as the righteous One. Put your hope in the Lord, not only for the trials of today but for the assurance that he will keep you until the end.

DAY 19

UGLY PRAYER AND THE GOD OF SLEEP

By Joel Fitzpatrick

Answer me when I call, O God of my righteousness! You have given me relief when I was in distress. Be gracious to me and hear my prayer! O men, how long shall my honor be turned into shame? How long will you love vain words and seek after lies? Selah. But know that the LORD has set apart the godly for himself; the LORD hears when I call to him. Be angry, and do not sin; ponder in your own hearts on your beds, and be silent. Selah. Offer right sacrifices, and put your trust in the LORD. There are many who say, "Who will show us some good? Lift up the light of your face upon us, O LORD!" You have put more joy in my heart than they have when their grain and wine abound. In peace I will both lie down and sleep; for you alone, O LORD, make me dwell in safety.

—Psalm 4

My alarm has gone off. I drag myself out of bed. It has only been a couple of hours since I laid down. Last night was haunted by the ghosts of my failure, past and present. Last night, I heard the voice of the accuser of the brethren reminding me of my sin and my shame. And yet as I wake up, sit at my desk and look out the window I am greeted by the sunrise. Blues, oranges, and pinks fill the sky, and I am struck by the beauty of it all, by the magnitude of it. God knew that I would have a rough night, full of doubt, full of fear. He knew that sleep would not come easily. So this morning, he kissed the sky for me. But last night, as I laid there in the dark, my heart was flooded with fear. I know God has forgiven me because he promised to (1 John 1:9; Isaiah 1:18). I know that he cares for me, that everything that happens is for my good and that he loves me to the end (Matthew 6:25-34; Romans 8:28-39; John 13:1). And yet, there I was in the dark wondering, "What will happen tomorrow? Will I wake up and remember? Will I be able to sleep tonight?"

This psalm is often referred to as an evening psalm and is supposed to read along with Psalm 3, a morning psalm. Where Psalm 3 speaks of the grace of God that sustains us in the morning, here in Psalm 4 we read of David's words as he lays down and sleeps.

He starts with this affirmation of the faithfulness of God, "Answer me when I call, O God of my righteousness!" David cries out with this cry, this ugly prayer. This is not the type of prayer that comes after a nice, easy day, where everything goes well. This is an ugly prayer. It is the sort of prayer that is not safe. It comes in the dark, in the middle of the night, when darkness is pressing in. This is not the sort of prayer that the pastor prays in church—you know, the safe prayers. God, heal this person. God, make that ministry go well. This is not the sort of prayer that we read later, prayers of sheer joy. No, this is the sort of prayer that gets prayed when you are laying on your side, in the fetal position, in a pile of tissues and a puddle of tears. Oh God, you are the one who has made me righteous. *Answer me.* Please, God, answer me.

David reminds himself of the nearness of God in the middle of his past suffering: "You have given me relief in the past when I was in distress. Now do that again, please. Be gracious to me and hear me!" Have you been in this sort of place—this place where all you have to hold onto is a distant remembrance of the deliverance of God? Notice, though, that this is exactly what David calls to mind. For David, it was less distant and yet here as he records this dark season, he calls to mind the work of God in the past.

He now turns to his accusers: "O men, how long . . ." David meets the accusations of those around him with the confidence that comes with the salvation that Christ gives him. John Calvin, the great reformer, says, "The sum is, that since God was determined to defend David by his own power, it was in vain for all the men in the world to endeavor to destroy him; however great the power which they otherwise might have of doing him injury."*

This is the hope that kept David through the night, this the hope that we have as we face those who accuse us. God has "set apart the godly for himself." He has done this through the person and work of Christ. Christ has come. He has lived the way you should live, he died the death that you deserve, taking God's wrath away from you, and then he was raised from the dead. In the middle of all of this, there was this incredibly important event. The curtain that separated humans from God, that kept God in the holy of holies, that very curtain was torn in two. God broke into the midst of our pain and allows us to bring our requests to him as those who are counted as "godly." This glorious truth is what gives you, dear believer, "confidence to enter the holy places by the blood of Jesus, by the new and living way that he opened for us through the curtain, that is, through his flesh, and since we have a great priest over the house of God, let us draw near with a true heart in full assurance of faith, with our hearts sprinkled clean from an evil conscience and our bodies washed with pure water" (Hebrews 10:19-22).

"Who will show us good?" (v. 6). Who will show you good, dear child of God? In the dark, in the midst of depression, in the middle of suffering and pain, notice what David says: "Lift up the light of your face upon us, O Lord!" This benediction language brings to us the comfort that comes as we live in the light of God's loving presence. In his presence is joy forevermore, more so than even a good harvest

---

* John Calvin and James Anderson, *Commentary on the Book of Psalms* (vol. 1; Bellingham, WA: Logos Bible Software, 2010), 40.

of grain and a lot of good bottles of wine. Again Calvin says, "The faithful, although they are tossed amidst many troubles, are truly happy, were there no other ground for it but this, that God's fatherly countenance shines upon them, which turns darkness into light, and, as I may say, quickens even death itself."*

Dear believer, are you waylaid by doubt and fear? Are you saddened by the way things go, the things people say? Can I encourage you to ugly pray, to come to God with all the brokenness of your heart? Then know that the "God of peace will be with you" (Philippians 4:9). Lay down and sleep, dear one, for God alone makes you dwell in safety. Those who accuse you cannot ultimately harm you.

---

* Ibid., 48.

DAY 20

YOU ARE NOT AS WHITE AS SNOW

By Daniel Emery Price

---

*Purge me with hyssop, and I shall be clean;
wash me, and I shall be whiter than snow.*
—Psalm 51:7

Hanging on to our sin is a terrible business. When it goes unconfessed, we usually try to double and triple down on it to keep it off the radar. Then we end up with far more than just the initial transgression we try to hide. And something happens to our conscience during our unholy charade. We stop feeling the weight of our sin. We are simply self-blinded to what we've done. And in the end, we tragically feel and see nothing.

David was in this position when he received a rebuke from the prophet Nathan. David had slept with his friend's wife, whom he got pregnant, then tried to cover it up, and in the end, he had his friend killed. How long did David hang onto these sins without confessing them? Long enough for a baby to be born. And long enough to no longer feel their weight.

So Nathan told David a story about a poor man who owned only a single lamb, which he loved like one of his children. One day his rich neighbor took the poor man's lamb and cooked it for his guests. David was enraged over this injustice and demanded punishment. In fact,

David wanted the rich man killed. At that moment Nathan unloaded four words that utterly crushed David—four words that exposed everything David was hiding. As David called for the execution of the rich lamb thief, Nathan responded by saying:

"You are the man!"

Nathan confronting David is a helpful narrative picture of what the Law does to all of us. It calls a thing what it is. It exposes the heart. It accuses us—every time.

I understand David's plight. I've been there. I've been named "the man"—and I pray you have too. It's the voice we all need to call us out and the hammer we all need to break us down. I'm grateful for Nathan. Without the matter-of-fact voice of the Law that he declared, we may have never received the gift that poured out of David after God gifted him with repentance. And we now have this treasury in Psalm 51.

I've read Psalm 51, prayed Psalm 51, and sung Psalm 51. As I recently read it once again, verse 7 jumped out at me. As David pleads for forgiveness, he makes an incredible statement. He asks for his sin to be purged—to be made clean. And then the verse states that if God washes him, he will be whiter than snow.

Did you catch that?

Not "white as snow" but "whiter than snow."

It's as if David is unable to find an example to accurately compare the purity that flows from God washing a sinner. The winter snow is the best example David can come up with, but it still falls short. You see, when sinners are forgiven—when they are washed—when they are baptized into the forgiveness and grace of God, they do not come out *white* as snow; they come out *whiter*.

The pure driven snow has nothing on the imputed righteousness of Christ.

The radical truth is this: when the Law comes in and rightly names us "the man" (as God repents us), Jesus enters the scene and states: "No . . . I am the man."

Jesus became every sin that condemned David, and he has become every sin that condemns you or me. Jesus became "the man" for the whole world of sinners. The cross of Christ is where perfection took away sin and sinners attained perfection. This cross is the gory and grizzly display of pure grace in which the world is declared righteous.

For every sinner/saint on the run.

For every transgressor in hiding.

Jesus has been named "the man" for you.

Come stand in the light. You're not white as snow. You wear Christ's righteousness, and that's a whole lot whiter than snow ever will be.

DAY 21

THE SHAPE OF GOSPEL ASTONISHMENT

By Jared C. Wilson

The earth is the LORD's and the fullness thereof, the world and those who dwell therein, for he has founded it upon the seas and established it upon the rivers.
—Psalm 24:1-2

There is God. He existed before anything existed, for he has always existed and he will always exist. He created everything that exists outside of himself, and therefore he owns it all, including humankind.

> **Who shall ascend the hill of the LORD? And who shall stand in his holy place? (v. 3)**

How can we enjoy fellowship with this awfully holy God? Who can justifiably enter his presence? The answer:

> **He who has clean hands and a pure heart, who does not lift up his soul to what is false and does not swear deceitfully. He will receive blessing from the LORD and righteousness from the God of his salvation. Such is the generation of those who seek him, who seek the face of the God of Jacob.** *Selah.* **(v. 4-6)**

Sigh. I would love to enjoy fellowship with God, to receive his blessing and his righteousness. But I don't have clean hands and a pure heart, and I have often lifted up my soul to falsehood and have sworn deceitfully. If that's the standard for acceptance unto God's favor, I can only hang my head in shame and sorrow.

> **Lift up your heads, O gates! And be lifted up, O ancient doors, that the King of glory may come in. (v. 7)**

What? What do you mean?

> **Who is this King of glory? The Lord, strong and mighty, the Lord, mighty in battle! Lift up your heads, O gates! And lift them up, O ancient doors, that the King of glory may come in. (vv. 8–9)**

Wait, what? Christ the Lord enters the equation? Well, of course! Of course *he* can do it! Jesus can abide in his presence, he can receive blessing from the Lord, he has a pure heart and clean hands, he is not false or deceitful in any way, and certainly he has sought the will of the Father at all times. I don't have to hang my head in shame any more: Christ my righteousness has entered and purchased justification before the holy God for me!

> **Who is this King of glory? The Lord of hosts, he is the King of glory!** *Selah.* **(v. 10)**

And hallelujah!

DAY 22

THE HIDDEN GOD AND MY HIDING PLACE

By Steven Paulson

Psalms 9 and 10 are mirror images and together explain the conundrum of a soul seeking grace from the Lord. Where does one look for this grace? Psalm 9 is the kind David would sing with his army after a great victory, "when my enemies turn back, they stumble and perish before your face" (Psalm 9:3). It is worth noting that you really do have enemies in life, and they are out to get you! This is not a misperception or merely paranoia, and when God brings these enemies down before you, you sing with David: "The enemy came to an end in everlasting ruins... but the Lord sits enthroned forever" (Psalm 9:6-7). God both "avenges blood" and maintains "my just cause" (Psalm 9:12, 4). What a great day when your enemies are rebuked, and the oppressed are set free.

Moreover, God's rebuke is not merely temporal but eternal. When God rebukes, the enemies pay with their own blood and are returned to Sheol (hell), where they belong (Psalm 9:17). Blood for blood, as the Law demands. But enemies keep popping up while you play whack-a-mole, and meanwhile, you must ask God for the grace that comes to the afflicted. Why does he let such enemies loose to wreak havoc in the world and me? What is this uprightness of the Lord that David seeks—that is, God's righteousness or justice? Of course, when David has just won a victory, the great justice of God is the Law. My enemies disobey the Law and oppress me. What, then, do I ask from God? I want my day in court, or my victory on the battlefield, and I want my enemies to suffer the consequences of their disobedience to the Law. So

David ends his victory over enemies with a prayer: "Put them in fear, O Lord! Let the nations know that they are but men!" (Psalm 9:20).

What David asked for is what any victor over enemies in battle wants: "Place a lawgiver over the nations, O Lord!" That is just what the Greek and the Hebrew mean in verse 20—give them a King and Judge—just as you, O Lord, are such a judge for me. God's justice on earth is the Law—and by it, the wicked who spill blood will have their blood spilled, and the oppressed will be freed. We need the Law and must have it—including in sermons in a church. What oppressors need is a lawgiver to oppress them.

However, God was not done with David, and now enters his strange work. Immediately after granting you victory, God hides himself from you and lets your enemies run roughshod again: "In arrogance the wicked hotly pursue the poor . . . boasts of the desires of his soul, the one greedy for gain curses and renounces the Lord . . . *his ways prosper*" (Psalm 10:2-5). Thus, we have the reverse view in the mirror of Psalm 10. But when God hides from us, we wonder if our enemy is really God himself: "Why O Lord, do you stand far away? Why do you hide your face in times of trouble?" (Psalm 10:1).

Indeed, why does God hide when we need him most? Why does he give us victory over the enemy one day, and then hide so that we cannot find him?

At the end of Psalm 10, when David says, "Arise, O Lord; O God, lift up your hand" in the face of the wicked who think God will never "call to account" (Psalm 10:12-13), the hope seems to be in God coming out from hiding to exercise the justifying Law. David then would depend upon the ultimate justice of the Law, even though it is presently hidden: "But you do see, for you note mischief and vexation" (Psalm 10:14). So, "Do justice!" (Psalm 10:18). Bring the Law. It is my only hope!

But God gives no relief in this way to David, until we hear something quite new and unexpected from this same warrior and king in Psalm 32:1: "Blessed is the one whose transgression is forgiven, whose sin is covered." Paul used this in Romans 4:6-8 as his evangelical discovery: "just as David also speaks of the blessing of the one to whom God counts righteousness apart from works." David no longer says, "Thank you for revealing yourself as my defender and destroying my enemies." Nor does he say, "Why are you hiding your face from me?" Instead, David now says the sweetest and most shocking thing, apart from the Law altogether: "You are a hiding place for me" (Psalm 32:7). The God whom I met without a preacher is either revealing nor hiding—but now, with a preacher, he has become my hiding place!

How does this happen that God becomes a hiding place? Apart from the Law, which God himself gives and uses for justice on earth, he now makes himself a place to run to—wrapped in the sermon of the word of forgiveness. God not only hides from me, but now lets me hide in him, since he has given a word David had never heard before: "I forgive you"—and look! His sin was covered; the transgression was blotted out.

So David pleads that you not be like a mule, who must be bridled (Psalm 32:9)—but instead listen to the preacher give the word of forgiveness. Then the *hiding God* becomes the *God who hides me* in his bosom. There no enemy, including myself, who can judge me otherwise. Even God will not judge me otherwise! In Psalm 32 David found the God who preached himself and so abandoned the search for an unpreached, righteous God. David was justified by God's promise, and nothing could assail him there. It makes all the difference as to whether you find God's grace in the Law, or in the gospel. David no longer had to seek God's grace/justice, because that justification now wrapped him in the Christ blanket, and he would never be exposed to harm again. For the time being God gives you a lawmaker, but when God hides, what you really need is someone to come and wrap you, hidden, in the Christ blanket.

DAY 23

PLANTED IN HIS GARDEN

By Cindy Koch

He is like a tree planted by streams of water that yields its fruit in its season, and its leaf does not wither. In all that he does, he prospers.
—Psalm 1:3

In the beginning of God's great story, he crafted an earth—a spoken creation inhaling God's breath of new life: light, water, beasts and birds, flowers and trees. In the beginning of God's great story, he gave this incredible gift to his finest creations: man and woman. Every plant and animal, day and night, sun and moon surrounded the most excellent of God's handiwork—his fleshly image walking around in the garden of Eden. In the beginning of God's great story, he placed his people there, resting them gently and firmly in the center of his love, as the apple of his eye. Our story of humankind began here, just as your prayers begin in the book of Psalms. Planted in his garden.

Our very first prayer in Psalm 1 digs right into the heart of who you are: blessed, the psalmist says, you are loved and favored by our great, almighty God. You do not walk with those wicked ones, you don't stand with those sinners, and you don't live with those who hate your God. The intensity builds, speaking of a separation from the unbelieving, unbeloved, unblessed people all around. Yet a quick ache of confusion makes me wonder who I really am. I have walked with wicked ones quite a few times. Whether I knew it or not, I listened to their counsel. I stand with the sinners, even defending their cause. I haven't spoken up when I should have. I stood back when God called me to action. I dwell with the mockers, living right next to their awful, hateful words. Am I the blessed one? Is this psalm even for me?

Our very first song in Psalm 1 presses down deep into the center of who you are. Blessed, the Psalmist says, you are righteous and faithful to our great, almighty God. You love the Law, the Torah of YWHW, God. You meditate on his Law, his Torah, every minute of the day and night. Every second of your time, every piece of your body and soul, is captivated by the Lord. Yet an honest twinge of guilt makes me wonder who I really am. I have forgotten the word of God. I have not let his word have its way with me. I even hate the Law of God, feeling condemned and ashamed when it gets too close. Am I the blessed one? Are these prayers even for me?

And you will hear of a great many answers to this question. Some may say, "Yes, you are blessed—but only if you can keep yourself away from those terrible sinners and your own wicked sin." Others may say, "Yes, you are blessed—but only if you can focus your heart, body, and soul on keeping the Law of God." Your best intentions and incomplete actions and terrible wickedness are mashed into a pitiful display before the great and almighty God. But it is the very next verse that frames your beginning in the book of Psalms.

> **He is like a tree planted by streams of water that yields its fruit in its season, and its leaf does not wither. In all that he does, he prospers. (Psalm 1:3)**

Unlike any preparation he can do to himself, here is the true beginning. The blessed one is "planted." The word in the original Hebrew text is passive. By no action of his own, he was taken from one place and placed in another, passively transplanted into a new beginning. Here, in fresh, deep earth, his roots will freely drink of lifegiving water. Having been placed in God's bountiful garden, here he will live. The blessed one will do what he was created to do—produce fruit, a natural gift from the creative voice of God. Each season, each day, each minute, he is budding with green leaves. This blessed plant, this blessed one, will never wither nor die.

Unlike any preparation you can do to yourself, here is your true beginning. You have been planted in the fertile soil of God's word. You have been carefully uprooted, purposefully transplanted, by no action of your own. The creative word of God even stretches your thirsty roots into his lifegiving water. Drinking in his Law, his Torah—his commands and promises and wonderful works from the beginning of creation. Drinking in his gospel—his promise fulfilled and completed and given to you by Jesus Christ. You have no other sustenance. There is nothing you can do but soak it in.

So, my friend, yes—you are blessed, transplanted into the promise by the life-giving blood of a Savior. You are firmly rooted among this faithful body of Christ. You are separated from the unbelieving sinners. You eternally delight in the Law, the Torah, of YHWH because you have died and risen with Christ.

In the beginning of this journey through Psalms, God places you, resting you gently and firmly in the center of his love, as the apple of his eye, in the righteousness of his beloved Son. This is your beginning—planted in his garden.

DAY 24

MY GOD, MY GOD, WHY HAVE YOU _____ ME?

By Chad Bird

My God, my God, why have you forsaken me? Why are you so far from saving me, from the words of my groaning?
—Psalm 22:1

On Good Friday, Jesus cried out from the cross, "My God, my God, why have you forsaken me?" (Matthew 27:46). He was quoting Psalm 22:1. When you hear those words, what do you think of?

That he's become sin so God turns his back on him?

That he's experiencing hell in our stead?

Whatever comes to mind, I'm willing to wager it's more influenced by the New Testament than the psalm from which it's quoted.

Quite frankly, I find that a wrongheaded approach. In fact, it's led to this square-peg psalm being shoved into a round hole of theology. Rather than leapfrogging to the New Testament, let's ask what Psalm 22 suggests those words mean.

When we look at those words in the context of the whole psalm, as well as in the original Hebrew, here's their thrust: this is the cry of one undergoing exile from God.

The sufferer is lamenting, "My God, my God, why have you exiled me?"

Three times, for instance, the psalmist complains of God being far away:

1) "Why are you so far from saving me?" (22:1—the same verse!).

2) "Be not far from me, for trouble is near" (22:11).

3) "But you, O Lord, do not be far off!" (22:19).

Just as Israel was exiled to Egypt, Assyria, and Babylon—far away from the holy land, far away from the face of Yahweh—so the Messiah is exiled from God.

The Messiah is recapitulating—doing over again in himself what Israel did. This happens throughout the ministry of Jesus. The Messiah lived in Egypt as a child as Israel lived there. He was tempted forty days in the wilderness as the nation was for forty years. He fed hungry people in the desert as Moses did for Israel. So on the cross he endured exile as they did. He was a refugee "far away" from God.

Just as Israel had the Babylonian exile, the cross is the Roman exile of the Messiah.

Jesus quotes the opening line of the psalm in Aramaic, the everyday language of his day, but the original is in Hebrew. In that language is another key to understanding the verse.

The verb translated "forsake" is *azab*. It's a word freighted with exile connotations. For example:

1) In Deuteronomy, God says that if his people forsake (*azab*) him by worshiping false gods, his anger will be kindled against them, and he will forsake (*azab*) them and hide his face from them (31:16-17). In fact, the only other place in the Old Testament where this exact Hebrew verbal form (*azabtani*) is used is when God says he will send curses (including exile) upon Israel because "you have forsaken me" (28:20).

2) In Jeremiah, God says that he has forsaken (*azab*) his house, abandoned his inheritance, and given his beloved into the hands of his enemies. Israel will go into exile in Babylon (12:7).

3) In 2 Chronicles, when Israel forsook (*azab*) the Torah, God sent the prophet Shemaiah to warn, "You have forsaken (*azab*)

me, so I also have forsaken (*azab*) you to Shishak [the king of Egypt]" (12:1, 5).

In other words, when the Israelites heard *azab*, they heard exile.

The Messiah is exiled from God on the cross as Israel was, forsaken as Israel was forsaken, cast away from Yahweh as Israel was. Why?

Interestingly, we usually say Jesus was forsaken because he became our sin (which is true! [2 Corinthians 5:21]). But Psalm 22 says nothing about the sin of the one praying. Like other psalms, it is the righteous complaint of one who protests to God because he is innocent, not guilty.

And that's the point! Psalm 22 is the plea of an innocent, righteous man who's treated like a guilty, unrighteous man. He is exiled even though his hands are clean. He is forsaken even though he trusts in God. He is cast away even though he clings to Yahweh.

Psalm 22 is the lament of an innocent man who undergoes what the guilty deserve. The focus is not so much on him becoming sin as it is on him being sinless but punished as if he is sinful.

Here is a man, fully alive, fully righteous, fully human, treated in a subhuman way. This prayer may be the most innocent, fully human expression Jesus ever uttered.

He is treated this way, however, so that when God hears his prayer, brings him back from exile, and draws him from the dust, the effect will be cosmic: "all the ends of the earth shall remember and turn to the LORD" (v. 27). His return from exile—in resurrection—will mean resurrection for all. "Even the one who could not keep himself alive," shall bow before God, shall eat and worship (v. 29). What Jesus experiences, all will experience in him.

Jesus's exile will mean Easter for the world.

Because Jesus prayed, "Do not forsake me," we know that God will not forsake us. The Messiah has brought us home from exile. He has made us fully alive in him. Never in Christ will we be far off from God, for in him God is not only with us, but he is one of us.

DAY 25

ANXIOUS, FEARFUL, AND RIGHTEOUS

By Bruce Hillman

For the righteous will never be moved: he will be remembered forever. He is not afraid of bad news; his heart is firm, trusting in the LORD. *His heart is steady; he will not be afraid, until he looks in triumph on his adversaries.*

—Psalm 112:6-8

When I first read these words, I am filled with a sense of disappointment. They don't seem to describe me, even though I wish they did. I've often struggled with anxiety and being responsible, and so when I hear that a righteous person isn't afraid of bad news, that they have a firm heart that trusts God, at steady heart that doesn't oscillate or fret, that this person isn't afraid and is ultimately victorious, I tend to ask, "Well, what I am I doing wrong?"

Verses like this tend to remind me I have a long way to go before I can call myself a "righteous person." In fact, part of my anxious spirit comes from overthinking, ruminating on every possible outcome, and trying to maintain a sense of control over things. I recall one time being in an Al-Anon meeting when another person said, "I spend most of my life living in someone else's head." That resonated with me because anxiety has an insatiable appetite for information—the curiosity anxiety brings often feeds its dark, unwelcoming reaches.

But verses like this require careful reading. Notice the tenses. The righteous *will never be moved*, they *will not be afraid* . . . These verses are promises of *future* hope because they present a vision of a person who lives by God's words. *If*—and it's a big *if*—we could live our lives as though God's word were true all the time, then these verses would be true of us—all the time.

Because we are both sinners and redeemed saints at the same time, we can never live perfectly by God's words. And yet scripture says, "the righteous shall live by faith." Faith continues to hold fast to God's words even as we are tempted to doubt them. More often we prefer to live our lives in the light of reason and experience. These seem more accurate and visceral to us. Faith is not opposed to these things, but nor does it submit to them either.

Living by God's words means continually asking, "Is this true?" about our feelings and frets. "I will never be happy again," "Everyone has abandoned me," "I can't be forgiven," "I'm just a failure." These statements represent *true feelings*, but *they are not true statements!* God says other things about us. He tells us that our joy is in him, that he will never leave or abandon us, that our sins are forgiven objectively because of Christ's work and that our failures can never separate us from his love, and that he wants to use us in his mission to save the world! How we *feel* is so often conditioned upon what we are experiencing. Faith grabs hold of something outside our experience, something objective and true that is not changed by circumstance.

So when we read the verses above, what we are reading is a vision of what we can be more like if we learn to listen to what God says about us over what our hearts say about us. We must walk in truth to gain the freedom of truth. We must walk by faith to have the sight of faith. And walking in faith is simply this—grabbing on to God's promises despite our changing moods and circumstances. Faith trusts, it gives the benefit of the doubt, it hopes, and it is ultimately defiant of any other narrative other than what God says about us. When we begin to practice this, we find God does the work of freeing us, and our hearts remain steady because they are not moved by every change and threat. Let us live in this promise.

DAY 26

GAZING AT THE GOODNESS OF ANOTHER

By Elyse Fitzpatrick

One thing have I asked of the LORD, and that will I seek after: that I may dwell in the house of the LORD all the days of my life, to gaze upon the beauty of the LORD and to inquire in his temple.
—Psalm 27:4

There have been times in my life when I must assume that I look like a goon, staring gape-jawed at something so overwhelming, so beautiful, that I have no words and just want to stare. Because I live within thirty minutes of the Pacific Ocean, I've often felt that way when watching the sunset. The golden sun breaks through clouds and beam shafts of light onto the ocean as it responds with sparkles and dances in the undulating rhythm of the waves. Even though I've seen a Pacific sunset more times than I can number, I honestly never tire of it. I'm sure I'm not alone. Whenever we see something beautiful, we just want to stare at it, which of course is why we buy paintings and take so many pictures. We know that the beauty we're seeing is something special, and we don't want to lose the experience of it. Somehow the experience of seeing beauty changes us.

Perhaps this is what David means when he says that he only has one prayer request: he wants to look at the beauty of the Lord and learn about him. Well, first of all, can we all just admit that if we only had one prayer request, it might not be to look at God's beauty or ask him questions? If you rubbed a magic lamp and a genie told you that you had one request, it could be anything, but you had only one, would this be what you'd ask for? Depending on the context, like if we're in church, we might think to say that, but is that really what we want most of all? Could we say it's just that *one* thing we want more than anything else? Would we even think of seeking God's face? Do we know why it would delight us if we did?

The Lord commanded David to seek his "face" (v. 8). In Hebrew, the abstract thought of someone's presence is always expressed with the word *face*. When God invites David to seek his "face," in essence he's inviting him into his presence to spend time with him. "Seek my face," the Lord requested. But it's actually more than than an invitation. It's an imperative, a command, a summons.

However you may feel about the president, if you received an invitation to meet with him or a summons to appear before him, you would probably feel both fear and excitement. That's because he has extraordinary power. You might wonder what you did or if you're in trouble, or how he might punish or bless you. But here we have the almighty God commanding David to seek him, to desire him, to spend time with him, and David responds with confident love: "My heart says to you, 'Your face, Lord, do I seek" (v. 8). How could David be so confident? How did he have the nerve to say, "Yes, Lord, I too want to spend time in your presence, before your face"? It is because he knows that his only hope is in God. He asks him not to send him away empty-handed, and he reminds him that he is his only hope of salvation or deliverance.

David confidently asserts and reiterates his trust in God when he says, "I believe that I shall look on the goodness of the Lord in the land of the living" (v. 13). He didn't think that God would kill him for coming into his presence but rather that he would sustain him. His mother and father might forsake him, but God would not cast him out or turn him away in anger (v. 9-10).

God's invitation and David's response should encourage us, too, because this isn't just an Old Testament thought, and David isn't the only one who was invited in. In 2 Corinthians 3:18, the apostle Paul writes,

> **And we all, with unveiled face, beholding the glory of the Lord, are being transformed into the same image from one degree of glory to another.**

Each New Testament saint who has looked to Jesus for salvation and deliverance is beholding him. Every time you say, "I'm trusting in Christ and all his work for me instead of in myself," you're beholding his beauty. Every time you hear words of absolution, "You are forgiven," or dine at his table, you're gazing on his beauty. Every time you pick up his word and expect to be made whole by it, you're spending time in his presence. You're standing face-to-face. And what does this do to us? It changes and transforms us to be more and more like him.

The experience of gazing upon beauty changes us. It makes us whole. Gazing upon Jesus transforms us to be more and more like the One whose beauty enraptures us. Feel free to enter into his presence today. You aren't changed by gazing at yourself. You're transformed by beholding his beautiful love for you. You've been invited in. You can say with David now, "I believe that I shall look upon the goodness of the Lord in the land of the living" (v. 13). Why? Because you already are.

DAY 27

SHOOTING AT THE SUN

By Donavon Riley

---

*The wicked plot against the righteous,
and gnashes his teeth at him.*
—Psalm 37:12

When we struggle and our faith seems to be eggshell fragile, it is often difficult to see God at work anywhere, especially not in our lives. When it seems that every moment of the day throws more temptations and afflictions at us, we wonder when God is going to step up and do something to help us. And why does God allow wicked people to curse and mock us? It even appears that wicked people, people who do not trust God or believe in him, catch all the breaks while we fight to just get out of bed each morning.

This is most true when we look at our brothers and sisters in the church. The smartest, most well-read, saintly looking people seem to do all right on their own without needing God's help. So does that mean those of us who wrestle and often lose to temptation, who fall into sin again and again, are God-forsaken? No, of course not. Even though we see pastors, theologians, and the "saints" apparently succeed at everything they do, do they rage against the gospel? If they are dependent on their own skills and abilities to gain God's favor, then they do rage against the gospel because the gospel tells us that the only true minister, theologian, or "saint" is one who trusts only in Jesus's saving work for us.

This is our great comfort, especially in suffering and trials. The righteous person is not the one who never struggles, never falls into sin, and is applauded for his saintliness. A righteous person is righteous because he trusts only in what Jesus does, and therefore God declares him to be righteous for Christ's sake. The enemies of the gospel lean on their abilities, skills, gifts, and strength. In fact, they end up trying to drive away the righteous because he trusts only in God's promises of forgiveness, life, and eternal salvation, not in anything he has done, good or bad. In fact, when we try to impress God with our doing, we are like a man who tries to bring down the sun by shooting at it with a pistol.

The true saint who clings to Jesus's bloody suffering and death for his justification will be the target of slander, cursing, gossip, false accusations, and the like. But only because he refuses to listen to others who encourage him to offer his words and works to God. Instead, a man who is declared righteous on account of Christ's work for him will be poor and in need more often than not. He will struggle, suffer, and be labeled all sorts of nasty things by people who are supposed to be his biggest supporters in church. And yet, this is what Jesus promises to anyone who listens to and follows him. When the false saint realizes he cannot climb up into heaven to kill Jesus a second time, he will go with the next best option: attacking and trying to kill our Lord's saints. And as Jesus himself says, they will believe they are offering true, acceptable worship to God when they do it to us.

The wicked are wealthy, powerful, influential, and generally happy people. And why not? They have everything they need. But the righteous are poor, often alone, and made to feel out of place in the church. What little he has, the false saints try to take away. But the psalmist encourages us (Psalm 37:16) not to be upset by this. Instead, leave them to their wealth, power, and happiness. It is better for the righteous man this way. They have piles and piles of family and friends and good things to fall back on in this life. But at the last day, they will encounter only God's disapproval of them because they confused the gospel of Jesus Christ with earthly rewards. But the one who is poor and in need, tempted and tried, in this life on account of his clinging to the gospel, at the last day he will be welcomed into the marriage feast of the Lamb that has no end.

Only trust in Jesus's saving work for us is of any lasting value in this life and into the new creation. God does not care about the size of our house, how many cars are parked in the driveway, how many friends surround us, or the number of people at church who call us "saint" and hold us up as an example of the God-pleasing life. None of that matters to him who says, "This is my beloved Son, with whom I am pleased. Listen to him."

God holds us up in all suffering and affliction. He will not let our faith be taken from us. He will not allow us to sink irretrievably into hopelessness. His arm and hand are over us and have an unbreakable grip on us. He loves us Jesus-much. And through faith in Christ Jesus alone, no matter how rough the going gets, we will be vindicated. God is on our side, so who can be against us? Who can overcome us? No one, because the One who overcame sin, death, and hell for us will never leave us or forsake and in him alone we live, move, and yes, even suffer the curses and condemnations of false saints because we trust that "God is a helper" and our "times are in your hands" (Psalm 31:15).

DAY 28

KEEPING HEAVY SECRETS

By Erick Sorensen

For when I kept silent, my bones wasted away through my groaning all day long. For day and night your hand was heavy upon me; my strength was dried up as by the heat of summer. I acknowledged my sin to you, and I did not cover my iniquity; I said, "I will confess my transgressions to the LORD," and you forgave the iniquity of my sin.
—Psalm 32:3-5

A while back I was watching my two oldest boys when my youngest told me, "Daddy I have a secret . . . but Mommy told me not to tell anyone."

So I said, "Okay, don't tell me."

"But don't you want to know?" he said.

"No, I don't want you to disobey Mommy by telling me. Just keep it to yourself."

This bugged my boy greatly. So a little while later, not being able to contain himself, he blurted out the secret. But then he said, "Now, Daddy, I can't tell my brother though."

I said, "Okay, don't tell your brother."

Two hours later I'm pushing them on the swings: "Hey, brother, do you wanna know a secret?"

Keeping secrets can be difficult! Keeping secrets about ourselves is deadly. No, really. A little while back a study from Columbia University was released and what it found "was that in four different tests, keeping a secret proved to have real—and perceived—physical effects."*

In the first test, Dr. Michael Slepian and his colleagues found forty people were told to recall a secret. They were then each asked to estimate the steepness of a hill. Those harboring a meaningful personal secret believed the hill was steeper than those who merely recalled little secrets. In another test, the researchers found forty people who admitted to recent infidelity. The participants first rated their guilt over the matter, and then they were asked to rate the energy and effort required to perform common tasks, such as carrying groceries upstairs, helping someone move, or walking the dog. The people who were more bothered by their secret rated the tasks as using more energy.

"The more burdensome their secrets were, the more participants perceived everyday behaviors as if they were carrying a physical burden," the authors wrote in the study.

The study's conclusion?

"The more burdensome the secret and the more thought devoted to it, the more perception and action were influenced in a manner similar to carrying physical weight."

Long before this study, the Psalmist already knew that holding onto our sins and secrets feels like carrying an unbearable weight. What's his solution?

Confession.

But oh how afraid of the consequences we are! We fear what others will think if they know what we really struggle with on a regular basis. The enemy of our souls causes us to wonder if God will still be faithful if we really come clean to him. So, like our first parents, we find any number of "fig leaves" to hide our shame and seek

---

* The Atlantic, Olga Khazan, Spill the Beans, July 8, 2015.

to carry our own sins to our own little cavalries. Before long, the weight crushes us. It is precisely at that point, when we recognize we can't walk anymore, that everything changes. With David, we remember again that our God is not a God who seeks us to condemn us, but to save us (John 3:17). We remember again that our God only helps those who *cannot* help themselves. We remember that Christ has already carried the burden and weight of our shame to the cross and has declared that we are forgiven once and for all of all our sins. And this means we never have to carry them again.

So today, whatever burden you're carrying, whatever sin your hiding, right now, come clean, admit it, confess it, and be free!

DAY 29

THE GOD OF REJECTS

By Jessica Thompson

We should take great care in observing how the psalmist relates to God. Our eyes and hearts should be open to seeing what the psalmist appeals to and how he addresses God. How does the sinner have communion with a holy and upright God? So often when we come to God, especially after we have screwed up, we want to point to past triumphs as our ticket for entry, or we point to how repentant we are. "See, God, I am really, really sorry." God will have none of our self-salvation projects when it comes to his grace and mercy. He will forgive for "his name's sake" or not at all.

In Psalm 25, the psalmist appeals to God's memory and to his character, and then he attempts to inflame God's compassion with the desperateness of his situation.

First, listen to the way he appeals to God's memory:

"Remember your mercy."
"Remember your steadfast love."
"Remember not the sins of my youth."
"According to your steadfast love remember me."

Now listen to the way he appeals to God's character:

"Good and upright is the Lord."
"All the paths of the Lord are steadfast love and faithfulness."

Last, observe the way he recounts his situation to God to inspire God's mercy:

> *"Turn to me and be gracious to me, for I am lonely and afflicted."*
> *"The troubles of my heart are enlarged."*
> *"Consider my affliction and my trouble."*
> *"Consider how many are my foes and with what violent hatred they hate me."*

Truly the Lord knows the psalmist's situation, the Lord knows the psalmist's past, and the Lord knows his own character, so why is it important for us to pray this way? The answer is of course for our own hearts. I need to be reminded every day of who God is, of who I am in relation to God, and I need to see the desperateness of my own situation. Once I see all of these things, I will gladly and wholly fall into the mercy of God. I will see how needy I am and how strong and able God is.

The Message paraphrase of verse 8 says this, *"He gives the rejects his hand, and leads them step-by-step."* What God is this, that gives himself to the reject? What God takes the hand of the one who no one wants? Our God—our God who understands what it means to be the reject. Our God who became man and was *"despised and reject by men; a man of sorrows, and acquainted with grief"* (Isaiah 53:3). The message of the world is to become a better you, to become stronger, more organized, healthier, wiser. The message of the psalmist is to see who you really are, a reject in need of a Savior. The lovely and heartwarming news is we have that Savior. We have one that understands our plight, who is near to the brokenhearted, who knows what it is like to be acquainted with grief.

So as you go to him in prayer and you pour out your heart to our God, appeal to forgiveness, appeal to his character, and tell him how desperate you are. There's no need to act stronger than you really are in the presence of the Lord. He knows. He sees. He loves.

DAY 30

BLURTING OUT PRAISE

By Joel Fitzpatrick

Praise the Lord, all nations! Extol him, all peoples! For great is his steadfast love toward us, and the faithfulness of the Lord endures forever. Praise the Lord!
—Psalm 117

There was a time in my life when I was able to eat hamburgers. Sadly, that time has passed. But when I was able to have burgers, I went to a local burger place and ate what they called the *Burger of the Gods*. It was amazing—so amazing that when the server came by to ask how I liked it, I told her that I didn't want to take another bite because the first one was so good, and I was afraid that the next would not be as good as the first.

In so many ways that is how it is for believers after they have experienced the love of Christ. There is no superscription to this Psalm, so we don't really know the context of it, but it is placed in the Psalter between two psalms that carry along the same theme, Psalm 117 stands as a burst of praise expressing in abbreviated form the love the God has for his people.

In its two verses, the theme is clear. When you get a piece of the unadulterated love of God all you can do is burst out with praise. In fact, the phrase "Praise the Lord" starts and ends this Psalm. The first encouragement to praise goes to the nations, the outsiders. Why would the Psalmist tell the nations to Praise the Lord? Notice, it is because God's love for Israel is so attractive. It is kind of like when you see an older married couple holding hands, expressing their love for one another, you are not the object of that love, but you can still be happy for the love they share. And, it can make you want a love like that.

This is what God's intention was, from Genesis 15 (Galatians 3:8f) to the giving of the law, through the prophets to the coming of Christ and the sending out of Paul the good news of the coming Messiah was a message for the nations. God's desire to show his love to the entire world is embedded throughout history. And that is exactly what he is doing. He is making the nations in v. 1 the "us" in v. 2. And he will continue to do that until the end of this age. Revelation 7:9 says, "After this I looked and behold, a great multitude that no one could number, from every nation, from all tribes and peoples and languages, standing before the throne and before the Lamb, clothed in white robes, with palm branches in their hands and crying out with a loud voice, 'Salvation belongs to our God who sits on the throne, and to the Lamb!'"

We are the nations! We are the goyim who now instead of having to experience the love of God from a distance, experience it firsthand. Why? Because Jesus has brought us into his Kingdom. Jesus has shown his everlasting love for us by laying down his life for us in order to break down the dividing wall and brought us near. We are the ones who are experiencing God's love and blurting out our praise. We are the ones who have experienced the steadfast love of God bubble over with praise for what he has done for us.

In this way, this little Psalm is the praise song sung by all those whom the Lord has called to himself. But it is also Jesus' Psalm. Jesus longs to be united with his people. He longs to have his church be filled with the nations and to be with him. He prays for it in his High Priestly Prayer, "Father, I desire that they also, whom you have given me, may be with me where I am, to see my glory that you have given me because you loved me before the foundation of the world." (John 17:24) For the life of me I cannot find the quote, but John Calvin said that in some way Jesus considers himself incomplete until he is united with us in paradise. He longs that we experience his faithfulness that endures forever. He longs to prove to us that death has lost its separating power over the Christian. He longs that we experience the faithfulness of God in the unifying power of the gospel here on earth as well as in heaven. And so, we unite together even now in praise because Jesus's love is really that good, and his faithfulness to his people endures forever.

As I have thought about this Psalm, its economy of words, and yet its overabundant praise, it has comforted my heart to think that these are the words we will sing, when we are in heaven. When we, with Christ, experience that completeness we will sing the praise of the Lord whose steadfast love endures forever. Praise the Lord!

DAY 31

THE LOST ART OF REST

By Daniel Emery Price

Return, O my soul, to your rest; for the Lord has dealt bountifully with you.
—Psalm 116:7

I have always found rest difficult. I'm one of those people who could easily fall into being a workaholic. Years ago, I hadn't been feeling well for an extended period of time, so I finally went to the doctor. He drew blood, tested my vitals, did a handful of other test, and then sat down and asked me some questions about my average week. Here was his diagnosis: "You don't get enough rest. You're otherwise completely heathy. But if you don't get more rest, you're going to kill yourself." No pills. No shots. The prescription I was given was, "You need to do nothing more often."

Spiritual rest (rest for the soul) is even more difficult than physical rest. It seems antithetical to "fruit bearing." Bearing fruit is something Christians spend significant amounts of time talking, writing, preaching, and arguing about. For many, it has become a wellspring of vexation. We ask, "How is my fruit? Am I bearing enough? Is it the right color and shape?" Sadly, we create all kinds of stress and insecurity out of something that is supposed to bring us comfort and peace. Fruit bearing is a promise from God we wrongly take upon ourselves to try and make good on.

Want a low-pressure statement? *"Apart from me you can do nothing"* (John 15:5).

If you can get past the initial offense of being pathetic, this statement from the lips of Jesus is incredibly freeing. I don't care how bad you want to bear some sanctified fruit; apart from Christ, it isn't going to happen. The fruit of the Spirit is called "the fruit of the *Spirit*" for a reason—it's his fruit.

Jesus calls himself "the Vine." That is, he is the only thing you must be connected to in order to have life. He and he alone is the source of any good fruit in anyone. And he says, "whoever abides in him *will* bear much fruit" (John 15:5)—it's a promise, an absolute certainty.

So the question isn't, "Am I bearing fruit?" Your question should be, "Am I trying to do something (anything) apart from Christ?" Lack of effort isn't the sworn enemy of fruit bearing. Self-sufficiency is.

Abiding in Christ is the only way fruit grows. And we try to turn it into a work we perform—which is the exact opposite of abiding. So you ask, "What does abiding look like?" Check out the story of Mary and Martha from the gospel of Luke.

> **Now as they went on their way, Jesus entered a village. And a woman named Martha welcomed him into her house. And she had a sister called Mary, who sat at the Lord's feet and listened to his teaching. But Martha was distracted with much serving. And she went up to him and said, "Lord, do you not care that my sister has left me to serve alone? Tell her then to help me." But the Lord answered her, "Martha, Martha, you are anxious and troubled about many things, but one thing is necessary. Mary has chosen the good portion, which will not be taken away from her." (Luke 10:38-42)**

That is what rest and abiding looks like: sitting and listening at the feet of Jesus. Abiding is staying put. And that's not a very demanding "one necessary thing." True rest will always be confused with being lazy or idle. Those with even the smallest amount of self-sufficiency refuse to be reduced to this kind of humble abiding. It's death to the old sinful, self-reliant us. We'd much rather be "distracted with much serving." The old Adam in all of us wants to escape from the feet of Jesus to help Martha wash the spiritual dishes.

The same Jesus who said, *"Abide in me"* also said, *"Come to me, all who labor and are heavy laden, and I will give you rest"* (Matthew 11:28). And these statements are not speaking about a contradictory paradox. Abiding *is* finding rest at the feet of Jesus. It's coming just as you are, hearing his word of pardon, and not leaving for some independent pursuit of sexier fruit.

If you'll stay put, God might just do something through you. He might even have a piece of fruit (or two) pop right out of you. In fact—he promises he will!

Lack of rest will kill you. But the psalmist has the prescription. Bid your soul to return to the restful feet of Jesus. He has dealt bountifully with us. There is no reason to ever leave.

DAY 32

WHAT SIN?

By Steven Paulson

Have mercy on me, O God, according to your steadfast love; according to your abundant mercy blot out my transgressions.
—*Psalm 51:1*

Psalm 51 teaches two things: mercy and sin. But aren't we already experts in sin? Why do we need God to teach it to us? Well, we are good at pointing the finger to say, "There is a sinner!" But it takes hard schooling to say, "I am a sinner—indeed nothing but sin ('in sin my mother conceived me' [v. 5]) and 'I only sin before you' (v. 4)." But what about my good created nature, my free will, my possibility for change? No. David is not a medieval scholastic or American evangelical. Thus, he learned all theology in one fell swoop: I, the sinner! God the justifier! There is nothing more you need to know.

Yet, the only thing that takes more schooling than my own sin is God's justification—because it is illegal. David already knew he was a scoundrel, as most kings are, but he didn't know that his real sin before God was his best quality—enthusiasm (trying to make God's word true, faster). David learned that sin is a matter of law and gospel, not law alone. So if you get your own sin wrong, you get grace wrong too. The old seminary teachers defined sin as anything said, done, or thought against the Law of God. Simple. That, in turn, made church repentance into a process of:

1. Thinking back over the past year.
2. Naming the specific sins.
3. Having sorrow over them.
4. Expiating them by "satisfaction" for the infraction.

This process tells me that my main concern as a Christian is to train my will's desires to want higher, spiritual things rather than lower, bodily things. Luther's teachers figured the will was good in essence (God doesn't make junk), but through malice, the will is misled, so a person may at best be able to keep the law in the act but always falls short of having the right intention. Thus, churches were there to improve our intentions. This is like telling a servant she isn't setting the table properly because she isn't dressed all in white while doing it—as if God requires the ten commandments . . . and then something more!

Instead, David actually started with the simplest commandment (coveting) and suddenly discovered he had broken the whole shebang: adultery, murder, false witness, stealing, dishonoring parents, dragging Israelites into war, and finally leading the enemies of Israel (the Ammonites) to blaspheme the first commandment because they conquered Israel so easily and took God to be "no god!" From one sin we learn them all. But then David found himself bereft of the one thing he needed: a preacher.

Nathan was sent by the Spirit to David (2 Samuel 12) and told David the tale of a man with "one ewe lamb," who treated it "like a daughter to him"—which was better than David ever treated God's promise. So Nathan caught David in the act. Of what? Not just pornography but denying the promiser—since the promise to David was directly attached to David's activity in bed. David's seed had a promise in it, and where he put it mattered to God.

Suddenly the true confession came out. David said to Nathan, "I have sinned against the Lord." But Nathan's job was not done. The next day the preacher came with: "Now the Lord has put away your sin; you shall not die." Then what? "Nevertheless, because by this deed you have utterly scorned the Lord the child that is born to you shall die." Yet, this was not God's need for satisfaction by law (a pound of flesh) but God refusing to let enthusiasts mess with his promise. God insists that the Seed be Christ. He chooses what Seed rules forever, when, and where—not David. He even let Bathsheba house the promise, since David himself was only the instrument. David must wait for Christ, not make his own Christ.

David's psalm begins, so full of the faith's surprising words that we cannot contain them all: "Have mercy on me, O God, according to your steadfast love; according to your abundant mercy blot out my transgressions" (Psalm 51:1). Faith always has these three sentences:

1. Have mercy!
2. On me!
3. O God!

How does David figure God will give this mercy *to me?* Not in my mind or in my will—but in my ear by hearing a sermon. And how will there be a sermon, unless there is a preacher? And how will there be a preacher, unless one is sent? And who will send one if not the Holy Spirit? O, how beautiful are the feet of those who come over the mountain!

David's sin was that he had no preacher. What to do? God sent a preacher who blotted out David's transgression so that if David ever went back to ask what happened to this sin concerning Bathsheba, Uriah, and the hidden God of majesty, the preached God would say: What sin?

DAY 33

THE WORD THAT MELTS THE COLD

By Cindy Koch

Praise the LORD, O Jerusalem! Praise your God, O Zion! For he strengthens the bars of your gates; he blesses your children within you. He makes peace in your borders; he fills you with the finest of the wheat. He sends out his command to the earth; his word runs swiftly. He gives snow like wool; he scatters frost like ashes. He hurls down his crystals of ice like crumbs; who can stand before his cold? He sends out his word and melts them; he makes his wind blow and the waters flow.
—Psalm 147:12-18

Praise the great Creator of the universe. Sun, moon stars, mountains, grass, flowers. God put each thing in its place from the beginning until now. Praise the winding, weaving road that he has given us. God leads us through valleys and over hilltops, across a wilderness praying the psalms through dark times and light. Praise the gifts from the almighty Lord that keep us going. People, promises, family, food, and strength. Praise the Lord.

However, this road has been long. Our journey in prayer has been almost too much. Cries of pain, laments, and sadness. Shouts of joy, relief, and comfort. A whirlwind of words collected for a God who loved and is loving his people in wonderful ways. A wasteland of waiting for a God who acted and who is acting now for his people in wonderful ways. Praise the Lord.

Like Israel wandering in the wilderness, and Jerusalem settling in the shadow of the temple, so we also struggle together to see the smiling face of our far-away God. Our psalms still search for the ancient Creator who first made us. Our prayers seek his stories of mercy and righteousness hidden among our daily hardships and joys. Our praises reach out to touch the distant God who has been enthroned in our ears. Praise the Lord.

We know he has acted. This is sure. God has strengthened. God has blessed. We remember this from the testimony of Israel, from the stories of Jerusalem, from the generations who tell about the mighty works of God. But it's more than just a story from the past. Today, he is still making peace, continually sending out his command. These verbs, recalling the mighty works of God, are participles. Making, sending, giving, hurling—God's actions are ongoing. His great salvation story, begun so long ago, is not over. We recall he did these things for our ancestors, but even today his word is still at work. Praise the Lord.

Continually acting, his word covers the earth like fresh snow. Every bit of his creation: mountain grass and flower covered in an icy blanket of the word. Every inch of our long road through the valleys, over hilltops, across the wilderness, is frosted over, trapped within his far-reaching, ever-speaking word. Touching everyone, every last cold and wicked sinner, God's word is hurling down from the heavens. The cold blast of God's voice overtakes us. Throwing shards of icy commands in every direction, God's command leaves us stiff and fearful, afraid. It freezes us, this unchanging, hard word of the Lord. Our unworthy, black heart is frostbitten and dead in the face of his bold, righteous word.

Who can possibly stand before his cold? Our psalms explore a heavenly God that we cannot control: ice, wind, waves, and snow. Our prayers can't harness his pure, solid commands that continually sting our flesh. Our praises can't stand the bitter winter wrath that our Lord still rains down upon the earth. We are left trembling, fearing, freezing. Who can stand up to his righteous, almighty cold?

But God sent out his Word. This particular time he sent his Word in flesh. A light that warms the darkness. A breath that melts the frost. A voice that will answer the cold and deadly question, *"Who can stand?"* And even though God continually covers his earth with daggers of icy Law, blameless and unchanging, God also sent his beloved Word to free this frozen and fearful creation. he sent out his only-begotten Word to reverse this cold, barren tundra where we are now trapped in prayer. He sent out a gentle, humiliating word of light to shine in the freezing darkness. Praise the Lord.

Only a Son of God could melt the wrath meant for the wicked. Only his perfect sacrifice could blow a breath of new life. Only a Word made flesh could exchange God's strict punishment, solid as ice, with fresh, living water. This great and amazing action of God does not remain frozen in the story of the past. Making, sending, forgiving—God's actions are ongoing. Christ is continually speaking, tangibly giving this forgiveness of sins for you. Praise the Lord.

In your calm baptismal waters, God is smiling at you on account of Christ, here and now. Christ's death and resurrection covered you completely by a splash and his name. In everyday words of ordinary people, the mercy and righteousness of Christ seeks after you, hidden among our daily hardships and joys. Christ finds you constantly with his spoken Word on the lips of others. In excellent physical gifts, the almighty Word, who has been enthroned in your ears, reaches out and washes over you, even today. Praise the Lord.

Praise the great Creator of the universe. Sun, moon stars, mountains, grass, flowers. God put each thing in its place from the beginning until now. Praise the winding, weaving road that he has given you. Praise the gifts from the almighty Lord that keep you going. But most excellently, God is making the word of Christ flow over you, continually. Praise the Lord!

DAY 34

THE LORD IS MY SHEPHERD, BUT I STILL WANT

By Chad Bird

The Lord is my shepherd, but I still want. I want whatever my heart desires.
He maketh me to lie down in green pastures, but I spy grass that is greener on the other side of the fence.
He leadeth me beside the still waters, but I know of still more exciting places where I'd love to drink my fill.
He restoreth my soul when I want to live life the way I see fit.
He maketh me to walk in the paths of righteousness when I want to run in the open fields of the world—eating where I want, sleeping with whomever I want, living like the beast I am.
He leads me for his name's sake, but I want to make a name for myself.
Oh the shepherd's rod is restrictive and his staff is stifling to my wandering heart.
Come valleys of the shadow of death, I shall not fear, for I know the lay of the land, I've been around the block, and I am the master of my fate.

So our untamed hearts sing. We don't want a Good Shepherd. We want a hireling, one who does not own us.

We crave our freedoms: freedom to walk in unrighteousness paths if the end justifies the means. Freedom to pull the wool over men's eyes, to twist every story to paint ourselves in the best light, to lie when we ought to confess, and to confess other men's lies to make our own wool seem that much whiter than theirs.

We are all sheep going astray. Let us return to the shepherd and overseer of our souls, for the freedoms we crave are slaveries in disguise.

The Lord is our Shepherd, our Good Shepherd. And all he wants is us.

I who so often turn my back on the fold and its shepherd? Yes, you.

I who have cursed his staff, ignored his call, gone my own way? Yes, you.

I who have been more like a wolf than a sheep? Yes, the Good Shepherd wants you.

Consider the heavens, the work of his fingers, the moon and the stars, which he has made. What is man, that he is mindful of him? All of us, that he cares for us? Yet for us, who are the sheep that love to wander, the Lamb of God is bound to the altar to bind us to himself. For us, whose mouths are open far too often, he did not open his mouth, like a Lamb that is led to the slaughter.

Have no fear, little flock, for he who is known by the Father knows us, calls us by name, and has made us his own. He gives us eternal life. We shall never perish. No one will snatch us out of the hands of the shepherd whose hands were bound to the cross.

He raises us from the pits we tumble into. He places us upon his shoulders and rejoices to carry us home. He washes us in cleansing waters, binds up that which is broken, and heals all our wounds. He prepares an altar before us and anoints our heads with oil. His cup continually runs over—over our lips, over our sins, quenching our thirst while making us yearn for more.

All this he does for us. And because he is the Good Shepherd, we are his good sheep. He gives his life for us. He makes our life his own and his life our own. He became what we are in order to make us what he is.

Surely goodness and mercy shall pursue us, shall precede us, shall be on our right and on our left, above us and below us, all the days of our life, and we shall dwell in the flock of the Lord forever.

DAY 35

GOD, I'M MAD AT YOU

By Bruce Hillman

With my voice I cry to the LORD; with my voice I plead mercy to the LORD. I pour out my complaint before him; I tell my trouble before him. When my spirit faints within me you know my way!
—Psalm 142:1-3a

How many times have you been mad at God? Probably more than you'd like to admit. I remember a time when a family member said some very hurtful things to me, and I was very upset. I felt the comments were extremely unfair and disingenuous. My mother gave me good counsel: "Bruce," she said, "hurt people *hurt* people." It is sadly true.

Sometimes in our close relationships, we have to be the dumpster people throw their trash at. Sometimes those closest to us will say the meanest things and treat us poorly because we are their safe people. Because love creates trust, loved ones become opportunities for hurt people to express themselves honestly because they know we won't leave or abandon them. So often we have to take the brunt of our lover's frustrations. Wisdom is needed here because relationships that do this with a manipulative goal are abusive. But often, *because* hurt people know you love them, they will say and do mean things to you. Just ask any parent.

When we are hurt, we cry out to God. But sometimes when the hurt gets really intense, our lament turns to complaint. Not only is this normal, but almost every lament in scripture contains a complaint.

Now it seems reasonable to me that if God included all these laments in his holy word, that was because he wanted us to pray them when we find ourselves in similar places. And if that is true, then essentially God is inviting us to be honest with him in prayer.

In this psalm, we see that affirmation. The psalmist pours out his complaint to God, telling the Lord his troubles and struggles. He is not afraid to be honest with God about what he is feeling. In fact, his spirit is so exhausted that he finds his only hope in the knowledge that God will set things right.

Sometimes we need to pray honest prayers. We must always pray with respect and reverence, but that doesn't mean we can't be honest: "Lord you have deeply wounded me. I am upset with you. Why won't you help me?" There is more truth and relational trust in that prayer than in the many prayers that ask God to "bless" and "give me this." Those honest prayers show that you trust God and love him, that he is your safe person, to whom you can continually come.

God himself demonstrated this love on the cross. When Jesus took upon himself the sins of the world, he also took upon himself the wrath of God against our sin. As he bears that wrath, he is forsaken *both* by God and humanity. He is the rejected One. Humanity has issued its complaint and finds him guilty; they nail him to a cross and reject him. God also rejects him on the cross-pouring judgment out upon him in the form of divine guilty verdict. The cross is the complaint of God against humanity meeting the complaint of man against God, the Man of Sorrows rejected by all. We hear his graphic loneliness: "My God, my God why have you forsaken me!" (Matthew 27:46). This cry, by the way, is not Jesus's own, but was first the psalmist's (Psalm 22:2). Jesus's words on the cross parrot human complaints. He speaks our words, takes our place, cries our desperation.

Because Jesus has taken our cause and our place, we can pray honestly. He himself complained, and he himself can endure it. The real challenge is not to let our complaints turn into ingratitude, in which case they can function to alienate us from God's love by puffing us up with entitlement. But on the whole, pray honestly. God will never abandon or forsake you. He is with you always—even when you are mad at him. Let us live in this promise.

DAY 36

FEAR AND TRUST, HAND-IN-HAND

By Elyse Fitzpatrick

When I am afraid, I put my trust in you.
—Psalm 56:3

Fear and trust: doesn't it seem like those two words don't belong together? I'm sure I've heard people say that it's impossible to trust in God when you're experiencing fear, but that's not what David said. David discovered a deeper level of trust in the midst of his great fears. He said that they go hand-in-hand.

When writing Psalm 56, David did so from a place of terror. When he wrote about being afraid, it wasn't some esoteric musing of what life might be like if circumstances in the palace weren't so cushy. No, when he wrote this song, he hadn't been made king yet, and he was in real trouble. First, he was on the run from King Saul, who, in a jealous rage, was marshaling all his forces to put David to death. As he escaped, David stopped at Nob, where the priests of the Lord were. While there, he asked for a sword and was given one: the sword of Goliath. Leaving Nob, David fled to the kingdom of Achish, the ruler of Gath. For David to flee to the king of Gath, carrying Goliath's sword, shows us just how desperate and terrified he was. Certainly David knew that he would be in danger there, having felled their champion. And sure enough, once Achish's servants recognized David, they warned him that David was a threat. David was "much afraid" (1 Samuel 21:12), so to avoid execution, he pretended to be mad. He feigned insanity and wrote on the doors of the gate and let his "spittle run down his beard" (1 Samuel 21:13). Have you ever been in such a precarious position that the only way for you to escape execution was to fake insanity? I haven't. But David was. He was terrified. His testimony was that his enemies trampled on him, and his attackers oppressed him (v. 1).

Let's reconsider now how David responded. First of all, he didn't pretend he wasn't afraid. David wasn't a wimp. He had been a hero in many conflicts. He had battled lions and warriors. But in this case, he was beside himself with fear. And he admitted it. We're wise when we do the same thing. It's not antithetical to our faith when we admit our fears. *Lord, you see my heart,* we can pray. *You know that I am afraid.*

The next thing that David did was to transfer his trust from himself and his own ability to escape death onto the Lord. *I will trust in you, Lord. I will believe your word is trustworthy.* He knew that every circumstance was stacked against him, but he also believed that the Lord was intimately acquainted with his situation: "You have kept count of my tossings; put my tears in your bottle. Are they not in your book?" (v. 8). David reminded himself that God saw him toss and turn at night; God collected all his tears. The Lord was there with him. He hadn't left him.

Then David made an astonishing statement. He said, "This I know, that God is for me" (v. 9). Somehow, in the midst of all his terror and humiliation, David knew that God's word was true, that he was "for" him, and that he could trust him. "I shall not be afraid," he said, and I'm sure at that moment, at least, he meant it. He believed that God would deliver his "soul from death" and his "feet from falling," so that he would walk before God in the "light of the living" (v. 13). His life would change.

How can we who are so frequently sinfully afraid, so weak and apprehensive, make statements like David's? How could we say that we know that God is intimately acquainted with our tears and fears? How could we assert that, "God is for us"? The only way that we can assure our own hearts is by remembering that our valiant King fought for us on the night he was afraid. Filled with fear at the prospect of receiving all of God's just wrath for all of our sin, surrounded by all the demons in hell, our faithful Champion, Jesus, said, "Not as I will, but as you will" (Matthew 26:39). He didn't feign insanity to escape the judgment due us. Rather, he walked clearheaded into the most excruciating terror and suffering ever known. He did this for us. So that now, we can say with confidence that he who is with us is, "greater than he who is in the world" (1 John 4:4).

Will there be times of fear, perhaps even times of terror in our lives? Yes, there will be. And this is our only confidence: we can know that his word tells us that he is the God who is with us, that he loves us, that he's intimately acquainted with all our grief, and we can trust in him. Join hands now with the One who bears the nail marks and say, "When I am afraid, I will trust in him." He has made an immutable oath: it is impossible for God to lie so that "we who have fled for refuge might have strong encouragement to hold fast to the hope set before us" (Hebrews 6:18). He sees it all, and he is for you. Anchor your soul in this sure and steadfast hope in the midst of all your fears. You will walk in the light of the living. He's promised it.

DAY 37

THE LORD'S FAVOR IS ON YOU

By Jared C. Wilson

Christian, God takes pleasure in you.

It's such a simple claim but such a difficult thing to believe, isn't it? Especially when it seems nobody else does.

Words sting. I have trouble to this day remembering encouragement given to me, even though I know I receive it regularly. I don't think this problem is all that rare. You likely suffer from it too. I can list quite easily the words that still haunt me.

A female classmate in my elementary school days calling me a "stuttering wimp" on the playground. A bully demanding I meet him after school to fight. A ministerial superior who once suggested I wasn't cut out for pastoral ministry. A worship leader at a conference where I was speaking informing me for some reason in the green room before I went out to preach that I wasn't the first choice for speaker. I could list an entire catalog of insults, accusations, and false claims accumulated from my fifteen years of writing online.

And then there are the ones that *really* hurt. Some are too painful to share publicly. Some are too profane. Some are water under the bridge, and forgiveness in these instances means not reminding people who may be reading of the pain caused. Some are just none of your business. But there's lots more, lots worse. And I'm sure you've been thinking of some things said to you too.

Some of the painful things said to us are malicious and some are not. Some are true things, some half-true, some not at all true. But they all hurt in their own ways, don't they? And the devil does one thing with these words: he turns them into fear and shame. The devil can turn even constructive criticism into a false accusation.

And then comes along this simple declaration from the one whose voice ultimately and sovereignly matters:

> [B]ut the Lord takes pleasure in those who fear him, in those who hope in his steadfast love. (Ps. 147:11)

The gospel clears the air. The gospel overturns the lies. The gospel wipes away the accusations. They may sting, but his word will endure forever.

The idea, in fact, that the holy God of the universe, the only one who has the absolute right to condemn us and dismiss us, declares his approval over us because of Jesus's taking our sin and shame is so wonderful, so hope-giving, so steadying. The almighty God takes pleasure in me. And you too.

Let them come with their words, then. Let the devil come with his barrage of lies, even his truths turned lies. We rebuke him. We confound him. We throw Psalm 147:11 at his sniveling little face.

The enemy comes with his wounding, haunting words, and I stand behind my advocate Christ the Lord. He gives me more words, better words, truer words.

As Luther reminds us:

The Prince of Darkness grim, we tremble not for him;
His rage we can endure, for lo, his doom is sure,
One little word shall fell him.*

Christian, the Lord's favor is on you. Ever and always. I won't tell you that what others say doesn't matter. You feel on the welts of your skin and the pain in your heart that they do. But we do know that ultimately, God's word matters more. And he will have the final say. He takes pleasure in you.

---

*   Martin Luther, "A Mighty Fortress," Public Domain.

DAY 38

THE HEAVENS DECLARE THE GLORY OF GOD (AND THAT'S NOT ENOUGH)

By Erick Sorensen

The heavens declare the glory of God, and the sky above proclaims his handiwork. Day to day pours out speech, and night to night reveals knowledge. There is no speech, nor are there words, whose voice is not heard.
—Psalm 19:1-3

Have you ever seen something so amazing, so awe-inspiring in nature that you almost felt like God was revealing himself to you in a more profound way? That's what David is expressing in Psalm 19. He is looking up to the heavens, observing God's universe, and is enraptured by it all. At this moment, in a certain sense, creation is like a book that "pours out speech" to us about who God is. Through the authorship of creation, God writes a letter to us, showing us how awesome and powerful he is.

In our day we have even more than the naked eye that David was limited to when he wrote this Psalm. We have such powerful microscopes now that one can look into the human cell and see our DNA. Norman Geisler explains,

> A single DNA molecule, the building block of all life, carries the same amount of information as one volume of an encyclopedia. No one seeing an encyclopedia lying in the forest would hesitate to think that it had an intelligent cause; so when we find a living creature composed of millions of DNA-based cells, we ought to assume that it likewise has an intelligent cause.*

Indeed, Romans 1:20 tells us that everyone naturally does "assume an intelligent cause" looking at nature: "For God's invisible attributes, namely, his eternal power and divine nature, have been clearly perceived, ever since the creation of the world, in the things that have been made."

David continues with his poetry:

> Their voice goes out through all the earth, and their words to the end of the world. In them he has set a tent for the sun, which comes out like a bridegroom leaving his chamber, and, like a strong man, runs its course with joy. Its rising is from the end of the heavens, and its circuit to the end of them, and there is nothing hidden from its heat. (Psalm 19:4-6)

David sees the glory and power of God merely from the sun's rising and setting on a daily basis. Indeed, this regularity, this constant predictability of the universe is one of the things that's always stumped skeptical philosophers. After all, how can we account for anything being predictable if this is an entirely random, unguided universe? As science has looked more and more into creation, some prominent skeptics have been forced to concede that there has to be Something above and beyond our universe. Consider the late philosopher Anthony Flew's story. For years, he was regarded as a premiere

---

* Geisler, Norman & Brooks, Ron. *When Skeptics Ask*. Grand Rapids: Baker Books, 1996. Pg. 21.

spokesman for atheism, so it shocked the philosophical and atheist communities when he suddenly announced that he had come to believe in some sort of divine intelligent being. In an interview, shortly before his death, he wrote,

> **There were two factors in particular that were decisive (for my conversion). One was my growing empathy with the insight of Einstein and other noted scientists that there had to be an Intelligence behind the integrated complexity of the physical Universe. The second was my own insight that the integrated complexity of life itself—which is far more complex than the physical Universe—can only be explained in terms of an Intelligent Source.***

And so God daily broadsides us with his abundant power and glory as we observe nature around us. And yet, as glorious as this book of nature is, it is not enough. If one merely gets their information about God solely from the book of nature or "general revelation," they won't get the full picture. Sure, they may see a powerful, intelligent Being, but they won't see the "God who so loved the world that he gave his only begotten son that whoever believes in him will not perish, but have everlasting life" (John 3:16). For that information, we must turn to the scriptures or the book of "special revelation." There, to our wonderful surprise, we find out that the God who made heaven and earth is intimately interested in our little planet. There, in the book of "special revelation," we find out that the God who is not bound by space and time, enters into space and time, becoming just like one of us (though without sin). There through the means of ink and paper, we see the omnipresent God subjecting himself to weakness, poverty, and eventually death to make payment for all our sins, raising to new life and ascending to the heavens in victory over sin, death, and hell. This holy God does all this because though he is the God who demands perfection (Matthew 5:48), he is also the God promises the justification of the ungodly (Romans 4:5). This God who is the Beginning

---

* To the Source, Exclusive Flew Interview, Benjamin Wiker, October 30, 2007.

and the End declares to all who trust in what he's done through Christ that they are forgiven sons and daughters, declared perfectly righteous in his sight.

So, the next time you see a beautiful sunset or have your breath taken away in praise on a starry night, remember the One who made all things isn't merely your sovereign, glorious God who governs and rules all things; he is your Father who sings over you with delight and joy.

DAY 39

COMING TO THE GOD WHO HEARS

By Jessica Thompson

Sometimes our confession before God is that we are not sure that he hears us. We are sure that if he sees us, he certainly won't forgive what he sees. We keep our distance. We look around for anything and everything to satisfy us that doesn't involve him. We are ashamed. We are broken. We are tired of giving into temptation and yet simultaneously still believing we will find some satisfaction in our sins. How could a holy God who sees and hears still decide to love, forgive, and satisfy? It is beyond our reasoning. We need faith. We need the work of the Holy Spirit to convince us that what the psalmist says in Psalm 65:1-4 is true.

> **Praise is due to you, O God, in Zion, and to you shall vows be performed. O you who hear prayer to you all flesh shall come. When iniquities prevail against me, you atone for our transgressions. Blessed is the one you choose and bring near, to dwell in your courts! We shall be satisfied with the goodness of your house, the holiness of your temple.**

When God gives us faith to believe verses 2 and 3, we will with confidence proclaim verses 1, 4-5.

"*O you who hear prayer, to you shall all flesh come.*" Our God hears prayers. I know that you are familiar with that sentence, but go back and read it. Now read this next sentence out loud. God hears my prayer. He is not deaf to your cries. He is not ambivalent about your heartache. He doesn't know the word *apathy*. He hears your prayers.

"When iniquities prevail against me, you atone for our transgressions" is an echo of Micah 7:18–19, *"Who is a God like you, pardoning iniquity and passing over transgression for the remnant of his inheritance? He does not retain his anger forever, because he delights in steadfast love. He will again have compassion on us; he will tread our iniquities underfoot. You will cast all our sins into the depths of the sea."*

It seems too good to be true, and yet it is the truest of all truths. This is our God. This God sees and chooses to trample our sins under his feet. This God knows and chooses to throw our sins into the depths of the seas. This God delights in steadfast love. Our God hears our prayers.

This is our God. Our God who chooses to bring us near. Our God who cannot stand to be in the presence of sin and yet made a way to encircle us in his arms. It is only good news to be drawn near to God when you know that you will receive welcome there. He not only draws you near, but he also welcomes you. *"This man receives sinners and eats with them"* (Luke 15:2). He not only receives you and eats with you but also feeds you with his very body broken for you. He promises to welcome us to our forever home: *"And if I go to prepare a place for you, I will come again and will take you to myself, that where I am you may be also"* (John 14:3). We truly are the blessed, the happy ones, the privileged ones, to dwell in his courts.

"We shall be satisfied with the goodness of your house, the holiness of your temple." Where else can we be satisfied but with him? Where else do all the longings of our hearts find their fulfillment yet in the goodness and holiness of his temple? As we go from one thing to the next looking for satisfaction, when we come to back to our senses as the prodigal son did, we will remember that there is only one place that brings us happiness.

And so as we remember all these things, as we rejoice in his atonement, as we see that he hears us, that he draws us near, that he satisfies us, we will then say with resounding conviction, *"Praise is due to you, O God, in Zion, and to you vows will be performed."* How can we respond with anything but devotion? May our hearts forever be drawn to such a good and gracious God.

DAY 40

UNITY LIKE BEARD OIL

By Joel Fitzpatrick

Behold, how good and pleasant it is when brothers dwell in unity! It is like the precious oil on the head, running down on the beard, on the beard of Aaron, running down on the collar of his robes! It is like the dew of Hermon, which falls on the mountains of Zion! For there the Lord has commanded the blessing, life forevermore.
—Psalm 133

When I was younger, I remember sneaking around to be able to watch the TV show *Cheers*. You know that '80s sitcom where everybody knows your name and they're always glad you came. I always identified with Norm—don't ask me why. Maybe because he was fat and had curly hair (and so did I). Perhaps because he always seemed to be snarky and yet funny at the same time. Who knows why. I was a kid. But it wasn't until I was an adult and going through seminary that this psalm began to stick in my mind. What I longed for then and what I long for now is a place where I am accepted and known and dwell with people who are glad I am there.

Here the psalmist paints a picture of the people of God dwelling in blessed unity. He gives us an idealized vision of the kingdom of God as something more than just the fragmented relationships that we encounter now. We walk in and out of churches, and we feel like outsiders. We don't fit in. We put on our church faces and act like our lives are put together, but when we leave, we realize that no one really knows us. This Psalm is a hope-giving Psalm, a Psalm of Ascent. It was written to be sung as the people of God walked to the Holy City, in unison.

King David wrote it. Put on your imagination hat for a second (if that is really a thing; I don't know, just go with it). David is sitting in his royal house, maybe on the rooftop looking at a procession of a million people walking and singing in unison all in anticipation of the holy days, all in anticipation of the celebration of God's deliverance, or God's protection, or the forgiveness of sins. And he can't control himself. "Behold, how good and how pleasant it is when brothers dwell in unity!" Even as I sit here in my small office, listening to Gregorian chants, I am struck by the beauty of a few voices singing in harmony with one another. Imagine millions of voices. Jaw-dropping beauty, joy-inducing music, brothers and sisters in unison, singing.

David likens it to really good-smelling beard oil. I love this metaphor because I have a beard, and I know how pleasant it is when my beard smells good. But this oil is a different sort of oil than just good beard oil. It is a deluge of a certain type of oil. In Exodus 30:23-25 and Leviticus 8:20 we read of this type of oil. It was anointing oil—oil that was used to consecrate Aaron for service. It was made of olive oil and mixed with very fragrant spices so that the smell would be sweet, and it was not to be replicated for common use. Why? Because God wanted the people when they came around their priests to smell the sweetness of the oil, the distinctiveness of this anointing oil. Now as a pastor I am very aware of the way I smell. Literally, it is a kind of neurosis of mine. When I go to hug people, I smell all sorts of things: coffee breath, sweat, leftover food, and cigarette smoke. Yet periodically when I hug someone and I smell them, it is a beautiful aroma. God is saying that when we dwell in unity, it is like hugging Aaron and smelling the sweet mixture of spices.

David then talks about Mt. Hermon and the dew that runs down and waters the land, bringing abundant provision, blessing, and fertile ground. Where the people of God dwell in unity, it brings these very things. We all long to be in a community of believers that gives us life and makes us feel loved and where we experience real, fruitful community. This comes as we announce the gospel to one another. This happens as we are known, our good and our bad, and we have people who speak the words of life into our lives. It happens when our brothers and sisters see our struggles, and they tell of the life, death, resurrection, and present intercession of Christ for us. That is like dew running down Mt. Hermon, bringing much-needed nutrients to our souls.

Last, we get this picture of heaven. The blessing, commanded by the Lord, is eternal life. As we dwell in unity here on earth, we experience in part what it is going to be like when we are in heaven. We experience the joy and warmth of deep communion. This last Sunday night, I was at church, and it came time to walk to the table and receive communion. We began to sing the old hymn, "There is a fountain filled with blood" acapella as we got in our lines and walked to the front. As I was walking to the front, it dawned on me, sinner and saint, young and old, addicted, struggling with same-sex attraction, transgender, proud, rich, homeless, highly educated, uneducated, healthy and broken, burdened and rejoicing, black, white, Asian, Hispanic, Indian, all were walking in unity, singing in unity coming to the very thing that unites us: Christ's body and blood.

It was in that moment, as we sang, "There is a fountain filled with blood drawn from Immanuel's veins; And sinners, plunged beneath that flood, lose all their guilty stains" that I was struck how by how good and how pleasant it was when brothers and sisters dwell together in unity. It was a little taste of heaven.

DAY 41

OVERCOMING OUR FOOLISH HEARTS

By Daniel Emery Price

The fool says in his heart, "There is no God." They are corrupt, they do abominable deeds; there is none who does good.
—Psalm 14:1

A few years ago, I came across a street preacher on the city square where I live. He had a decent-sized group of people gathered around listening to him, so I decided to stop and catch an ear full. "The Bible says that you are a fool if you're an atheist!" the man shouted. "You're all fools!"

On the one hand, he's right; that is what Psalm 14 says. But I couldn't help but think of Jesus's words in the Sermon on the Mount: "Whoever says, 'You fool!' will be liable to the hell of fire" (Matthew 5:22). I suppose I understand the temptation to stand up and call yourself wise and everyone else an idiot (isn't this why social media exists?). But what Jesus says there ought to give us pause. Jesus's words don't mean there are no fools but rather that there are only fools and hypocrisy is damnable. That day the city square was occupied by only fools, myself and the preacher included.

When David says "The fool says in the heart, 'There is no God,'" he is speaking about everyone. He is talking about himself and the whole of the human race. This is made clear when he follows that statement with: "The Lord looks down from heaven on the children of man, to see if there are any who understand, who seek after God. They have all turned aside; together they have become corrupt; there is none who does good, not even one" (Psalm 14:2–3).

God has searched the earth looking for one person who "understands" there is a God and who "seeks after" that God. But he has found no one. Not you. Not me. Not David. All he sees is an all-inclusive mess of selfishness, corruption, and fools pretending to be wise. So what does God do? He sends someone who believes in him to save us. He sends himself.

Jesus is the one who has not "turned aside" and "does good." But we don't want a God so unlike us. So our foolish hearts cry out, "Crucify him!" In this crucifixion, Jesus (the one who was not "corrupt") became the corruption of the world to save it. Jesus died to redeem a world of unbelieving fools, and through the preaching of this message, he overcomes our foolish hearts.

We are tempted to think "believing" is the thing we've done that separates us from all the fools. But nothing could be further from the truth. Faith is a gift from God. It's not flashy or boast-worthy. It's total dependency on the God who saves utter fools and only utter fools.

I confess, I still hear my heart whisper, "There is no God." I sometimes live like I am my own God. I sometimes look at others and think, *What a fool*. It turns out my foolish heart is still being overcome by the love of the God it fights against. I may not be wise, but perhaps, like David, I'm just wise enough to know I'm a fool in constant need of being overcome.

DAY 42

WHAT THE PEOPLE OF GOD WILL BE (AND ARE!)

By Jared C. Wilson

Psalm 48 is a wonderful exultation in God and ought to serve as a kind of master anthem for the community of faith. The city mentioned is a foreshadow of the church, the body of Christ made up of all sinner-saints, and just as in these precious lyrics, the hallowed renown of God is to begin and rise up from the worship gathering of our sacred assembly and spread out in our daily missional presence in the world. The influence of the church upon the world is first and foremost to be about the worship and magnification of God, the heralding with passion of his glory and splendor, and the proclamation that he reigns and rules forevermore in Christ.

So what does Psalm 48 tells us the church should do and be like? More than a few things:

1. The church should bring joy to the world (vv. 1-2). As salt and light, graced people bring hope to a disgraced world.

2. The church's message is that God is a fortress, a refuge in times of trouble (v. 3). The only hope for people who have rebelled against God is God himself—specifically in the freely offered righteousness of Christ, our Rock and Redeemer.

3. The church makes it clear that Jesus is Lord over and above all lords, and she leads with the radical call to a revolutionary kingdom that challenges and usurps worldly authorities and

systems (vv. 4–5). We subvert worldliness and rebel against rebellion by following our gracious Savior as the king whose subjects are truly, finally, eternally free!

4. The church is forthright about God's holiness and righteousness, which provokes repentance and the fear of the Lord (vv. 4–8). Contrary to the opinions of some, the commands of the Lord are not burdensome to those who have been set free from the condemnation they announce for those who do not know God. So we preach the bad news as if it is truly, terribly bad, so the holiness given to us through the good news would be seen as truly, terrifically good.

5. The church is known for the love of God. They meditate on God's love, even (v. 9). Because if we do not love, we do not know God. But because we do know God, we love not just him but our neighbor as ourselves. If the church does not exhibit God as love, they show they do not know God and thus aren't even the true church. Because God doesn't just have love; he is love.

6. The church's zeal for the glory of God, for the proclamation of his fame, for the spread of his praise, spills outside the city walls and flows to the end of the earth. The church does not exist for her own ends, for her own maintenance, but for the glory of God and the good of the world. The church, to put it simply, is on mission (vv. 10–14). And this mission is primarily to announce the greatness and lovingkindness of God demonstrated most abundantly in the gospel of Jesus Christ's sinless life, sacrificial death, and glorious resurrection. In an age of increasingly consumeristic religion, there is no greater "mission statement" than this.

7. The church cultivates a legacy of God's faithfulness (v. 14). In other words, we serve a God who weds himself to us not because we are faithful but because *he* is. He will never leave us or forsake us. Imagine if the church treated others with the preemptive, unilateral, unconditional grace God has shown us. Wouldn't that speak to the faithfulness of God much more than

our religious busywork or legalistic leveraging? We worship a God who never gives up on us. He is faithful. Let the church believe it.

Psalm 48 as a portrait of a gospel-centered church is an incredible song to reflect on. Clearly we're not there yet. But God *is* faithful, and despite what anyone thinks of the church, Jesus has promised that the gates of hell will not prevail against it. When I think of that, when I think of God's faithfulness to us, when I think of Jesus's love for his bride, and when I take those thoughts and run them through great anthems like Psalm 48, I cannot help but think of how the church can and will be (and, dangit!, often *is*) radiant with the glory of God.

DAY 43

HE PREACHED, AND IT STOOD FIRM

By Steven Paulson

Shout for joy in the Lord, *O you righteous! Praise befits the upright. Give thanks to the* Lord *with the lyre; make melody to him with the harp of ten strings! Sing to him a new song; play skillfully on the strings, with loud shouts. For the word of the* Lord *is upright, and all his work is done in faithfulness. He loves righteousness and justice; the earth is full of the steadfast love of the* Lord. *By the word of the* Lord *the heavens were made, and by the breath of his mouth all their host. He gathers the waters of the sea as a heap; he puts the deeps in storehouses. Let all the earth fear the* Lord; *let all the inhabitants of the world stand in awe of him! For he spoke, and it came to be; he commanded, and it stood firm. The* Lord *brings the counsel of the nations to nothing; he frustrates the plans of the peoples. The counsel of the* Lord *stands forever, the plans of his heart to all generations. Blessed is the nation whose God is the* Lord, *the people whom he has chosen as his heritage!*
—*Psalm 33:1-12*

The first thing we say about God, in both the Apostles' and Nicene creeds, is that God is almighty: "I believe in God the Father almighty." Almighty is not so much an attribute as part of God's name. After all, if your god is not almighty, you had better find one who is, or you are wasting your time. When I pray, I want to contact the God who can actually do something. But of course, there is a reason we say we *believe* in almighty God, since reason and every fiber of our being fights against this truth of God's almighty power. We want God to be pretty mighty but to leave enough room in the universe for humans to have a space where we are perhaps not mighty but at least have enough power to affect our fate in the end. This dream seems to help us fend off the fear that God does everything by divine necessity and leaves nothing to our human wills. But then we are overcome by the fact that we can't ever seem to be faithful to God. We are weak, and so we are forever at loose ends.

Almighty God refers to omnipotence or power. But when sinners think of power, they can only imagine power in terms of the order, structure, and beauty of the law. Does someone have the wherewithal not merely to think about something, but to act—not just to talk the talk, but walk the walk? In fact, thinking this way considers that spoken words are the least powerful thing on earth: "sticks and stones may break my bones, but words may never hurt me." But unlike creatures, God's power is actually in his *word*. One of the most difficult and frightening cases of God's word-power is the scripture that says: "God hardened Pharaoh's heart" (Exodus 9:12). Luther recognized that God not only hardened pharaoh's heart, but God does *everything* in the universe by his eternal word.

To show how important this is to the preaching of the gospel, Luther turned to Psalm 33: "For he spoke, and it came to be; he commanded, and it stood firm" (v. 9).

Even the powerful King David had to command someone to do something and then wait to see if would happen. Who knows? It depends upon the will of the servant. But David was finally made sure by the time of his thirty-third Psalm that God had only to speak to him—even once—and instantly everything was already done. It had happened to him that way through his preacher Nathan.

God's all-working, almighty power is done purely by speaking, and it travels at the speed of sound.

The whole of Psalm 33 is David giving thanks to God for this one thing: He speaks to me! God opened his mouth and gave me His word! O, wondrous day! So, David gives a yelp of joy (v. 1) in the form of a "new song" that is directly contrary to what David thought power was like before he got a preacher. For that reason, since David never liked singing alone, he wants you to sing with him with brash shouts and loud guitars (v. 3). God preached to David, and David could not help but rejoice. Who would not praise this sermon vociferously, once the silent, mysterious, and fearful God opens the heavens and actually says something to you? And what God says is not, "How is the weather?" or "What are you doing for me?" but rather "The word of the Lord is *Yashar*—Joshua/Jesus" and all his word/deeds are done "in faithfulness." No wonder David was so happy. He thought he was going to get a full condemnation when God spoke, but he got Christ/mercy instead.

Then David put together the two things most important about God's word. First, "By the word of the Lord the heavens were made" (v. 6). In the beginning, before anything was made that ever was made—God spoke and it came to be. This is what we call the doctrine of *creation* concerning God's almighty power. Then, second, when God finds a sinner (like David) and gives his promise of forgiveness to him, he instantly becomes a *new creation*! Justification of the ungodly is a new work done by God's word alone.

So what about you? If God ever forgives you, it is not just allowing you to start over and try harder the second time, but it is a whole, new, complete justification that is given as a free gift and without any work of my own—outside the law. This is especially a work that is not done by any exercise of my free will (or Pharaoh's). Creation and justification, these two doctrines, are what God does with his word. Furthermore, the second is so new that it cannot be corrupted, changed, or lost because, "when God speaks, so it happens, as he commands so it is" (v. 9). What the Lord promises, he faithfully delivers (v. 4). And no power in all the world (not mine, not Satan's, not the nations') can overcome it: "The LORD brings the counsels of the nations to nothing;

he frustrates the plans of the people—the counsel of the Lord stands forever" (v. 11).

Faith eagerly anticipates what God is going to say again, since he has now chosen us (v. 12), and no person or power—height or depth—can separate us from the love of God in Christ Jesus. What he promises he necessarily, faithfully, delivers. Go ahead and sing this new song with David.

DAY 44

BLAMELESS AND BLESSED

By Cindy Koch

---

*Blessed are those whose way is blameless, who walk in the law of the L*ORD*! Blessed are those who keep his testimonies, who seek him with their whole heart, who also do no wrong, but walk in his ways!*
—Psalm 119:1-3

Blessed? That must mean those other people walking along; they have it all together, they found the proper path. They do it the right way. Blameless, sinless, perfect people. Nice and polite, loving and generous, beautiful and successful. Those who walk the walk and talk the talk. Those who keep the Law of God and love him with their hearts, souls, and minds. Blessed, here, must be those others.

"You have commanded your precepts to be kept diligently" (v. 4).

Because you, God, are holy. You demand perfection—the best of one's heart and mind every second of the day. Every effort must be directed toward you glory. You expect blameless actions, sinless lives, perfect love. And you have commanded this holy standard for your people. Those whom you love should follow your laws. Those whom you chose should listen only to your commands. Those whom you made into your people should walk eternally in the Law of the Lord.

"Oh that my ways may be steadfast in keeping your statutes! Then I shall not be put to shame, having my eyes fixed on all your commandments" (vv. 5-6).

Oh! How I wish my path was straight. How I may lie to the others that my way is right. Oh, how I wish I could just be perfect. It's what you want. It's what I want. But I slip away from your blameless presence. I always seem to backslide away from your holy law. I've endured until now, but my horrible standing still shames me before you. Yet there you stand, Lord, commanding me to follow when you know I can't.

"I will praise you with an upright heart, when I learn your righteous rules. I will keep your statutes; do not utterly forsake me!" (v. 7).

But I hate this Law of the Lord—blameless, sinless, perfect Law. Because in the middle of the night, in the depths of my own soul, I know this is not really me. I am jealous of my beautiful neighbor. I want to steal his glory and fame. I am tired of being the good Christian everyone thinks I am. I am exhausted from hiding the wickedness that churns inside. I have failed to love and help others who need it. I live my life selfishly for my own happiness. I do not let the law of the Lord direct my life as it should. Will I ever get better? When will I not be put to shame? How do I learn your righteous ways? I beg you, Lord, do not abandon me just yet.

"Blessed is the man who walks not in the counsel of the wicked, nor stands in the way of sinners, nor sits in the seat of scoffers; but his delight is in the law of the Lord And on his law he meditates day and night" (Psalm 1:1).

Blessed? Is this how I keep my way pure? A man who does not walk or stand or dwell with sinners. Blessed? Is this how I clean up such mess of a walk? A man who lives saturated in the word of God day and night. Blessed? This is not describing who I am! I want to be this blessed one—but I am not able to go all the way. Every time, every place, every day, every night? Who can possibly be blessed under the flawless Law of the almighty God? Blessed? A man who does nothing for himself and perfectly loves those others. Blessed? A blameless, sinless, perfect man. There is only one man who lives up to this: Jesus Christ is the blessed One who prays these words, not me.

"I will praise you with an upright heart, when I learn your righteous rules. I will keep your statutes; do not utterly forsake me!" (v. 8).

And so, I don't hate the Law of the Lord. Blameless, sinless, perfect Law. Because in the death and resurrection of Jesus Christ, he gave the completed and finished Law to me. He was beaten for my weakness, he bled out for my wicked desires. He endured all the way to death, forsaken for my petty, selfish problems. He suffered for my failures and gave me his victory. From beginning to end, the Law of the Lord was praised, kept, and filled by Jesus. And there you stand, Lord, commanding me to follow, smiling at your perfect Son you see in me.

Oh! That my ways may be steadfast in keeping your statutes! Then I shall not be put to shame, having my eyes fixed on all your commandments.

Oh, how his path was straight. Humiliating, dirty, yet his way was completely right. He was exactly what the Father wanted. Weighted with the sin of the world, he returned victorious to God's blameless presence. Never did the Son of God forsake God's holy Law. Never did the Son of Man avert his eyes from the path of commands. This man is the blessed One, unashamed to stand up to God's Law, for me.

"You have commanded your precepts to be kept diligently."

You, God, are holy. You demand perfection. The best of One's heart and mind every second of the day. Every effort directed toward you glory. Blameless actions, a sinless life, perfect love. And you have commanded this holy standard for your people. You have been pleased by the holy actions of your Son. Those united with Christ follow your laws. Those who live by the word of Christ listen only to your commands. Those crucified and raised with Jesus walk eternally in the laws and promises of the Lord.

"Blessed are those whose way is blameless, who walk in the law of the Lord! Blessed are those who keep his testimonies, who seek him with their whole heart, who also do no wrong, but walk in his ways!"

Blessed? Those are the people killed with Christ. They have it all together, and he raised them to new life on his proper path. They take comfort in his right way. Blameless, sinless, perfect people, cleansed, forgiven, renewed. Nice and polite, angry and rude, loving and generous, cranky and stingy, beautiful and successful, wretched and suffering. Jesus kept the Law of God and exchanged it for your unworthy heart, soul, and mind. Blessed, here, is a merciful gift won by your Savior. Blessed, on account of Christ, are you.

DAY 45

PRAYERS SPLASHED WITH THE BLOOD OF THE CROSS

By Chad Bird

Jesus is always many things: always truthful, always faithful, always divine. But he is not always nice.

He wasn't nice to the religious goody two shoes when he nicknamed them white-washed tombs or when he told Peter that his speech reeked of hell's halitosis. And remember that time he compared a distraught mom to a dog begging for table scraps?

No, Jesus is always many things, but he is not always nice—not always rainbows and butterflies.

Sometimes Jesus is mean and brutal and cold and downright harsh. Some encounters with him leave us singing, "What a foe we have in Jesus."

And this is good. The worst thing that could happen to us is always getting the Jesus we want. That Jesus gives a thumbs-up to our every decision. He affirms us no matter how stupid we become—a kind of spineless, boot-licking savior whose sole objective is to cheer us on as we sprint like Usain Bolt down the track to hell.

If you find your Jesus agreeing with every decision you make, let him be damned because hades is his home. An always nice, always agreeable and affirmative Jesus is nothing but the devil in a savior suit.

What makes this so hard for us to accept? We think one-dimensionally. We suppose that if Jesus is our friend, he can't be our enemy. If he is loving, he can't be harsh.

But God's Son is infinitely more than our fragile egos have flattened him out to be. As no true friend would stand idly by while we guzzled poison but would slap the cup out of our hand, so Jesus has been known to strike out. To shake us up. To get in our face. Indeed, to drag us kicking and screaming away from spiritual suicide so he can talk life into us once again.

In other words, Jesus has been known to Psalm 88 us.

Psalm 88 is Psalm 23 after it's been run over by a truck. In this psalm, the Lord is my wolf. I am in want. He makes me lie down in the grave. He rejects my soul. When I walk through the valley of the shadow of death, I fear every evil, for I am alone. It's that kind of psalm. Raw, bloody, R-rated. It's the kind of psalm we pray when it feels like Jesus has become our enemy or we his doormat.

Psalm 88 is the only lament psalm where there's not tiny pinhole of light at the end of the tunnel. It's pitch black. Our lives draw near to Sheol. We're like the corpses in the grave. God has stripped us of hope, friends, and even life. He has rejected our souls. Hidden his face. Turned a deaf ear to our prayers. Here's how the psalm ends: "You have caused my beloved and my friend to shun me; my companions have become darkness" (Psalm 88:18). Darkness—that's literally the final word.

This is the kind of psalm we sometimes need because this is the kind of God we sometimes have. The one who, judging by every outward standard we have, every sense we possess, every bit of reason we exercise, hates our guts.

And it is to this hateful God that we pray. We pray against God to God. We pray against our enemy by praying to our friend. We pray from the darkness and hopelessness of a life gone terribly wrong to the only one who can save us—even though he's the very one who's put us there.

Jesus is the friend of sinners and the foe of sinners. His friendship necessitates his enemyship. He is a God who kills to make alive, wounds to heal, so of course he's got to wound and kill us before we vacate the tomb.

The road to Easter never bypasses Golgotha.

But here's the thing: to truly know God is to recognize him in suffering and the cross—to feel like Jesus is your foe but to believe, despite a mountain of evidence to the contrary, that he is your friend, your very life. Christ's greatest work among us will always be splashed with the blood of the cross—messy and dirty and confusing. But it must be this way. The labor of love that God performs in us often hurts like hell. In fact, he often executes our dreams and hopes so we might die and rise to God's dreams and hopes for us.

Jesus isn't always nice. But he is always truthful and faithful, which is far better. What's more, he's walked our path, however dark and dismal. A Savior who cried out that his Father had forsaken him on the cross is a Savior worth believing in. Compassion and sympathy are as deep as the marrow in his bones.

So when we cry out that he's forsaken us, he nods and says, "Yes, so it feels. But I haven't. I'm on the cross with you, dying with you so I might carry you out of the tomb on Easter morning."

What a strange friend we have in Jesus. But he's the best friend any of us can have. Because when our eternity is at stake, when life itself hangs in the balance, he'll rush into the thick of the fight, with eyes blazing with the fires of a divine love for us that will never, ever go out.

DAY 46

YOU CAN'T WORK FOR PEACE

By Bruce Hillman

It is vain that you rise up early and go late to rest, eating the bread of anxious toil; for he gives his beloved sleep.
—Psalm 127:2

Sometimes the hardest part of the day is the time just before sleep. At that time, if struggles or stresses abound, we can be kept up by racing thoughts. This fretting and over-analyzation, the frantic search for options, can leave us exhausted and depleted, feeding the cycle of stress that is already at work in us.

King David knew this struggle well. If he seems condescending or trite with his advice in Psalm 127:2, it is only because he has been victimized by racing thoughts so many times before. When he was younger, Saul, the king at that time, put a death bounty on his head and hunted him. Frightened and alone, David knew no other place to hide then in the dangerous terrain of the desert. How bad do things get when you go to the harsh environment of the desert for safety? Alone, confused, terrified, and feeling abandoned, David knows he needs his strength for the coming struggles. That strength is dependent on rest, something he finds impossible to attain. No sleep adds to the stress and makes it more difficult to sleep in a dangerous pattern of unwellness.

In Psalm 3 David records his thoughts at that time. He says that in his moment of trouble, God was a shield-wall all around him, protecting him. He then writes, "I lay down and slept; I woke again, for the LORD sustained me. I will not be afraid of the many thousands of people who have set themselves against me all around." What a testimony! God's care has produced faith that has sustained David to the point where his fear is turned to rest. This is not dissimilar to our Lord, who reminds us to come to him in our weariness to find the rest we need.

Psalm 127:2 offers a critique of the "Protestant work ethic," which promises success from hard work. It condemns the view that what is needed to be safe, happy, and at rest is conditioned upon human effort. We must be careful not to miss the point. David is not saying that work is bad or that no effort is required on our part to achieve a fruitful living. Rather, he is calling out the notion that hard work achieves peace. It does not. We cannot work our way out of our problems. We cannot simply try harder or hustle more. This doesn't mean we should be irresponsible or lazy but that we should firmly understand the limits of hard work's benefits. Hard work can lead to some form of mastery and worldly success. But not always. And it never can give what all hard workers are working for: peace, happiness, and joy. Work is always a means to these ends, and in that sense, it is utterly incapable of delivering.

David tells us that working for peace and rest is *vain*. That's another word for "foolish" or "meaningless." Because peace is a gift and not a product, you can't work your way into it. However—you can *receive it by grace.*

Jesus is our Prince of Peace. He is Immanuel, "God with us." Only he can offer the rest we need. Jesus can offer this rest because he was the man of sorrows for us. He treads the path of sin and death, hell, and damnation so we can be free of its curse. The eternal consequences of our sin, the everlasting haunt of death and hell, are no longer threats to us. Because Jesus has defeated these threats by walking our path for us, and because he has shown us a new way, that is himself, we have been given the gift of peace. That is why, traditionally, at church people will greet each other in "God's peace."

Jesus's peace is not as the world gives. It cannot be taken away by bad circumstances. Perhaps you find that hard to believe. Perhaps one reason why that is the case is that you are set upon working your way out of your struggles. What if God's peace was different? What if God's peace, instead of rescuing you out of every trouble, was so powerful that you no longer feared going through it? That is the promise of Psalm 23, where we hear that we, "walk through the valley of the shadow of death." Not around it—through it. Why? "Because we fear no evil!" Why? "Because he is with us." That is godly peace. It is not a buffer from all wrongs but a present God of peace that is not intimidated by life's worst. After all, he has faced the worse, for us, and he has won.

God's peace is simply this: whatever may come, and whatever may happen, whatever you may lose, and whatever you may endure, it will be okay. It will be okay because he is with you and gives your faith promises to grab hold of.

May his peace be yours today, in each fragile moment. Let us live in this promise.

DAY 47

THE RESTORED SOUL

By Elyse Fitzpatrick

The law of the Lord is perfect, reviving the soul . . . Let the words of my mouth and the meditation of my heart be acceptable in your sight, O Lord, my rock and my redeemer.
—Psalm 19:7, 14

Have there ever been days when you felt crushed, so broken that you just can't seem to lift up your head? Sometimes we feel that way because circumstances or people around us have deeply disappointed us. Perhaps you've just received bad news from the doctor or maybe you learn that people you love dearly are facing financial ruin. I've lived nearly seven decades, and I've known significant times of crushing and brokenness. Or maybe you feel this way because you've gotten, once again, another glimpse into your own heart and your lack of faith and disobedience make you feel you can hardly breathe. I know what it's like to feel pathetic like that, too.

In light of what we know about David, both his successes but especially his failures, what he writes in the second half of Psalm 19 is astonishing. He writes, "The law of the Lord is perfect, reviving the soul" (v. 7). When I read that, I have to wonder what Law he's talking about. Sure, I'll acknowledge that the Law of the Lord is perfect. Of course it is. As a display of God's character, his Law is perfect and holy and good. His word is complete, lacking nothing, utterly true. Yes, God's word is perfect.

But—and this is the part that I have to wonder about—how does his perfect Law *revive* me? How am I supposed to look at the perfections of God's character, decrees, and instructions and be revived? How am I supposed to say, "Oh, that's so beautiful. It brings life to my soul. It *restores me*"? Honestly, I'm more prone to say that it crushes me. It tells me all the things that I should be doing (and aren't) and all the things that I shouldn't be doing (and are). It strips me naked and makes me ashamed of myself. That's not what I would call revival.

How is it possible for David to look at the perfect Law of the God who demands a perfectly righteous life, and say, "Oh, I love that! It's a beauty! It's a delight!" How could I possibly say that?

This is one of those places where if we fail to read the Psalms as Jesus instructed his disciples to, we'll miss the passage's meaning. On that first resurrection Sunday, Jesus taught his disciples how to read the Psalms. He said, "These are my words that I spoke to you while I was still with you, that everything written about me in the Law of Moses and the Prophets and the Psalms must be fulfilled" (Luke 24:42). So the Psalms, and in particular this psalm, in some way has to be about Jesus. And if that's true, then I am not only invited but also instructed to read this verse and the ones that follow it, with the good news about Jesus in mind. And it's then that "the Law of the Lord" begins to revive my soul.

God's Law begins to restore my brokenness and bring me to life when I see all its perfections and am forced to run to and rely on the mercy of Christ. In its most primary form, God's beautiful Law is meant to crush me and thereby free me from all of my self-deluded self-confidence. Instead of trying to prop my soul up with foolish affirmations about my innate wonderfulness, it tells me that I've got nothing. And in doing so, it actually frees me to come alive in the only way that's possible: with the perfect life of Christ. It forces me to look to the only One who ever said (and didn't lie when doing so), "I always do the things that are pleasing" to God (John 8:29). The only Person who ever lived who actually loved God's Law the way it should be loved is Jesus and it's only in giving ourselves to him by trusting, relying on, and resting in the work he's done that we can find our souls revived or restored.

The sole way that all the crushing that happens in this world can be reversed is by the knowledge that we don't have to rely on ourselves and our goodness ever again. When difficulties happen (and they certainly will), we can know that the Lord will restore our broken souls. The gospel tells us that, if we trust in him, we've been made alive by the Word who became flesh and lived like one of us (John 1:14). It was this Word who also walked out the Law every moment of his life. He did it for us. We, the simple, have been made wise, our hearts are made to rejoice, and our eyes have been enlightened (Psalm 19:7-8). And this news is so good, it tastes like honey. It's worth more than all the riches the world can offer (v. 10).

Knowing that Jesus has perfectly fulfilled all God's gorgeous Law in my place frees me to invite God to look into my soul, to convict me of sin, because I know who I am and who he is. He is my Rock and my Redeemer. How can the words of my mouth and the meditation of my heart be acceptable in his sight? Because he is my rock, redeemer, righteousness. And because of that, I can stand in wholeness and boldness with restored soul and say, "Yes, Lord, your Law is perfect, and through it you have revived me. Help me to respond in gratitude this day and every day."

DAY 48

SINNERS WHO LOVE RIGHTEOUSNESS

By Donavon Riley

You have loved righteousness and hated wickedness.
—Psalm 45:7

In the Bible, the word *righteousness* is shorthand for "believing in the Savior who is Jesus, and loving God and our neighbor." Righteous describes faith and works. It means we trust God to be God for us and loving our neighbor as a gift. However, so we do not assume this is about our doing, it is all accomplished in and for us by the gospel. God's grace, not our efforts, distinguish righteousness and unrighteousness. We are "in Christ through faith," as St. Paul describes our relation to God, or we are not in Christ. Both the righteousness of faith and the righteousness of works are the fruit of the gospel, which is at work in and through us.

When the psalmist writes that God loves righteousness, he is pointing to the Christ, and when he says God hates wickedness, he is pointing at us who do not do the good we desire but are always pursuing the evil we do not want to do. In this way, the psalmist lays out for us that God is only pleased with us and can only declare us righteous, and all sin will be permanently forgiven and forgotten when he looks at his Son, whose blood covers us in his righteousness. Only as the gospel works in us to create faith and produce good works can we say that for Christ Jesus's sake we are righteous. We are not righteous because we do righteous work, but we are righteous because Jesus has done the work already and through faith in him he declares his work is credited to us. Then, in relation to Jesus, God declares his love for us. We are acceptable to God only for Jesus's sake. Left to ourselves, there is nothing of our doing that is not wicked. Even the things we imagine are our very best efforts are a damnable sin to God. This is why we may lose everything, even our lives, so long as we are held firmly in Christ Jesus's steadfast love for us, who is our forgiveness, life, and eternal salvation.

Now the world wants nothing to do with the gospel of Jesus Christ, especially when Christians explain that we may give up everything, lose everything, suffer everything so long as we enjoy the love of God in Jesus Christ. How could something as weak and powerless as words communicate all the treasures of God to us? If Jesus is God's Son, the world's Savior, why do we still suffer? Why do we still die? Why is there so much pain and hurt? Why is there so much lawlessness and godlessness if the gospel is the power of God unto salvation for all who believe?

What the world does not comprehend is that the righteousness of God suffers himself to be rejected by the very people who he came to save from their sin and death. That he is God's own Word born in the flesh. That the same Word that created light and dark, man and woman, law and gospel, takes our place on our cross and dies our death for us. He descends into our hell for us and is raised from our grave so that sin and death and hell may have no power over us. The world does not comprehend that the gospel is the good news that all the hurt, pain, suffering, death, and hell that await us were trampled down and finished by Jesus for us. What is left of hurt, pain, suffering, death, and hell is our sad attempts to strip Jesus of his glory, glory that is lifted up off the earth, stretched out on his cross, for all the world to see on Calvary.

The crucified Christ is God's sign and banner that no one is righteous, not one. All have fallen short of the glory of God. All need the blood of the Lamb to cover their sin and rebellion. Only Jesus is righteous, and we, therefore, can only enjoy righteousness in relation to God if Jesus declares us righteous for his sake. It is on account of Jesus's work for us that we are declared righteous, not because of anything in us or anything we have done to prove to God we are righteous.

We Christians are then called lovers of righteousness because we are in Christ through faith. Jesus alone is our righteousness. We are loved by God for Jesus's sake. We are righteous in all we do because we are in Christ Jesus, even when it does not sound or look all that righteous. We are righteous because God declares us righteous for Jesus's sake, not because we speak or act in a way the world considers righteous. Without Jesus, without the relationship he establishes with us through his gospel and gifts, we are godless outlaws and wholly unrighteous. But now, in Christ through faith, God sends his preacher to announce to us that Good News that it is all accomplished and done for us, that we are lovers of righteousness because Righteousness has loved us.

DAY 49

VENTING (TO THE GLORY OF GOD)

By Erick Sorensen

How long, O LORD? Will you forget me forever? How long will you hide your face from me? How long must I take counsel in my soul and have sorrow in my heart all the day? How long shall my enemy be exalted over me?
—Psalm 13:1-2

I don't know about you, but when I go through something difficult, I find myself wanting to vent. Sometimes I vent to my wife, sometimes I vent to a friend, and sometimes I even vent to God in prayer.

But is that okay? Is it acceptable to vent to God? I have come across people who say no. Stressing our need to go to God with reverence and fear, they imply that expressing raw emotion is not proper for a true child of God. In fact, many of us have been made to feel bad or less than Christian if we dare voice our deepest disappointments to the throne of heaven.

Well...

This idea just doesn't square with scripture. The fact is, a great deal of God's word is filled with venting from many of God's faithful followers. We call them "laments." David fills the Psalms with such emotional outbursts (one of many, many, many examples is listed above). Jeremiah weeps in agony in his Lamentations. And Job all throughout his ordeal even goes so far as to beg God to take his life, complaining about the seeming unfairness of it all. Far from being offended or embarrassed by our laments, I would dare say God invites us to bring our deepest laments directly to him. Over and over again we are charged to come to God with "pure hearts." One way of reading that word *pure* is to say "holy." And that would be fine. But part of what it means to be holy is to approach God without a façade—without a mask on. It means to be honest. It means "calling a thing what it is."

I mean, really if God is God, who do we think we're fooling anyway? Our omniscient God isn't fooled by our fake piety any more than he was duped by Adam and Eve's fig leaf shorts. God would rather have us venting honestly than faking it deceitfully.

I'm reminded of a scene from the movie *The Apostle*. Sonny, an itinerant preacher (played by Robert Duvall), has just found out his wife is cheating on him and his life is really going to pot. So he starts praying:

> **I'm gonna yell at you because I'm mad at you. I can't . . . take it! Give me a sign or something. Blow this pain out of me. Give it to me tonight, Lord God Jehovah. If you won't give back my wife, give me peace. Give it to me, give it to me, give it to me, give me peace. I don't know who's been fooling with me, you or the devil. I don't know. I won't even bring the human into this. He's just a mutt anyway, so I'm not even gonna bring him into this. But I'm confused. I'm mad. I love you, Lord. I love you, but I'm mad at you. I. am. Mad. At. You! So deliver me tonight, what should I do? Now tell me, what should I do?***

In my mind, that's grade A venting!

But let me get back to the rebuttal mentioned at the beginning: those who say we should not vent because we should approach God with fear and reverence have a point. I mean after all, how is it that us unholy brats can expect to come to God with our complaints and not be swiftly rebuked, judged, and condemned?

---

* The Apostle, Robert Duvall, October Films, 1997.

Here's how: no matter how you bring your prayers, your laments, your complaints to God, in the final analysis, the reason why this holy, perfect, righteous, and entirely just Lord can deal with that venting is that ultimately it is covered by his Son Jesus Christ.

The good news for us is that we don't approach God merely on our own in our own strength, our own eloquence, or our own theological accuracy, but we approach God being completely covered by the ongoing intercession of his Son. We go to God under the substitution of his strength, his righteousness, and his eloquence.

Check this out: the Bible says in Hebrews 7:25 that Jesus *"always lives to make intercession for us."* Do you hear that? There is never, ever a moment at which you are not covered by him. Why does he do this? Because as 1 Timothy 2:5 says, he is the "one mediator between God and men, who gave himself as a ransom for all." And so Romans 8:26 says, "the Spirit helps us in our weakness." Why? "Because we don't know what to pray for as we ought." So we're told, "the Spirit intercedes for us with groanings too deep for words and according to the will of God!"

Your venting is acceptable to God because the Spirit and the Son make it acceptable to God. As 1 John 2:1 tells us, he is "our advocate" standing by our side, speaking in our place. He is our translator before the courts of heaven so that our honest ranting and venting aren't heard merely as the complaints of a sinner but as the request of a beloved child.

DAY 50

WHAT WE NEED, EVERY DAY

By Jessica Thompson

Currently, I am sitting in a rocking chair at my grandma's house. She is sleeping. Another cat nap in the middle of the day in an attempt to ease her troubled mind. My uncle, who is her primary caretaker, is having triple bypass surgery as I type these words. She is worried, obviously. But more than that, her mind is failing, and she cannot retain any information. So she asks again and again what is going on with him, and if he is okay, she pleads for information that she knows she will soon forget. She has a general sense that all is not well and that he is in the hospital, but the fact that she talked to him last night escapes her. She is abundantly kind and apologetic as she starts in on a question that she has already asked me several times in the last few minutes. My heart hurts for her as I repeat my answer over and over and over again. I don't mind repeating myself as I see the worry ease just a bit from her face, knowing full well we will repeat the process in less than five minutes. She needs the sought-out answer. She needs it now, and she will need it five minutes from now and again in a few minutes.

> I must hearken to the gospel, which teacheth me, not what I ought to do, (for that is the proper office of the law,) but what Jesus Christ the Son of God hath done for me: to wit, that He suffered and died to deliver me from sin and death. The gospel willeth me to receive this, and to believe it. And this is the truth of the gospel. It is also the principal article of all Christian doctrine,

> wherein the knowledge of all godliness consisteth. Most necessary it is, therefore, that we should know this article well, teach it unto others, and beat it into their heads continually. (Martin Luther, *St. Paul's Epistle to the Galatians*)*

Luther said that we need to beat the gospel into our heads continually. The psalmist in Psalm 143:8 also echoes this sentiment when he says, *"Let me hear in the morning of your unfailing love, for in you I trust."* The Psalmist is aware of his continuing need to be reminded of God's unfailing love. Every morning may it be our first thought. "I am loved unfailingly by God." This thought will undoubtedly lead to the next part of our verse, *"for in you I trust."* His love inspires our trust. Then the psalmist goes on to say, *"Make me know the way I should go for to you I lift up my soul."* The next part of our prayer is that he would guide us. That his unfailing love would be a bright beacon throughout our day. That the knowledge of his love would inspire us to return that love and to love his people.

You see, our minds are weak, and like my grandma, we need continual assurance. We need to hear every morning, afternoon, and evening that despite our performance for the day, we are loved. We are loved with an unfailing love—a love that is beyond comprehension. And the really crazy part is God doesn't get fed up with our continual asking, doubting, wondering, if he still loves us. I know for me there are certain days when I look back on my day and I think surely he couldn't love me after what I did or failed to do that day, but the answer, again and again, is that he loves his children. He will continue to love his children. He doesn't mind at all telling us again. So with the Psalmist, we cry out, *"Let me hear in the morning of your unfailing love."*

---

* Martin Luther, *St. Paul's Epistle to the Galatians* (Philadelphia: Smith, English & Co., 1860), 206.

DAY 51

DANCING WITH GOD

By Joel Fitzpatrick

Sing praises to the LORD, O you his saints, and give thanks to his holy name. For his anger is but for a moment, and his favor is for a lifetime. Weeping may tarry for the night, but joy comes with the morning.
—Psalm 30:4-5

God is pretty wild. He is in the business of flipping things over. God takes impossible situations and with the twist of his hand turns them around. Psalm 30 is such a great picture of this reality.

It seems to me that when we go through long periods of suffering, we can tend to think that all of life is that way. Depression settles in like an old, unwanted friend, and there can seem to be no way out of it. Maybe you just can't see how God is going to work in the middle of your situation—a job loss, a friend who is suffering, the death of a loved one. These periods of midnight are scary and come to us in unexpected seasons. We all will affirm, in theory, that this life is a life of suffering, and yet we are still surprised when that suffering skulks into our lives.

David was a man after God's own heart, and yet he was also a man who suffered. Suffered from the oppression of Saul and Absalom. Suffered the results of his sin with Bathsheba, the death of his son. Suffered from depression (Psalm 32). David suffered. But he was also a very proud man. And God is a very kind God. He was with David through the suffering. Even in David's pride, God was there.

This psalm takes us through the warp and woof of David's existence and tells a tale of hope—hope that comes through the reality that our God is living, active, *and present*. This psalm was written looking forward to the construction of the temple. It looks to a time when the visible sign of the presence of God in the midst of Israel will be constructed. But remember, the temple was not constructed until after David was dead, and yet we read the song he sang in anticipation of this momentous occasion.

He surveyed his life, and he came to the conclusion that we all should come to: without God we are in deep trouble, but when God shows up on the scene, there is deliverance and blessing. This is so encouraging to me. Many say that this psalm was written at the end of David's life after he committed one of the most egregious sins in his life, a self-serving act of pride akin to Nebuchadnezzar's sin. David numbered the people, and in doing this, he brought God's judgment on Israel. God gave him a choice, and David chose three days of pestilence to come on the people of Israel (2 Samuel 24).

Now we read this song of praise for the dedication of the temple. God had come as judge, bringing pestilence on the land, David offered a sacrifice, and God forgave them. Now you may be wondering why this matters to you.

Look at the psalm. David's weeping was over the reality that the sin he committed cost so many Israelites their lives and had brought great sickness on him. He says, "Oh man, I really messed things up this time. I have been brought to the doorstep of Sheol. But you, God, have restored me" (Joel unauthorized paraphrase). Have you been here? You are experiencing the temporal consequences of your sin, and you wonder if God's discipline will ever stop. You wonder if your sadness will ever go away. Here are these words of hope and rejoicing. God's anger is not yours forever. It will not be on you for the rest of time. Why? One commentator helps us to understand it by saying this,

> **The forgiving mercy of God towards his own people is expressly pointed out in verse 5 as the *kernel* of the Psalm. It is very**

> remarkable that previous to the laying of the material foundation of the temple, this should have been pointed out by God Himself, as the spiritual basis on which the temple was to rest.*

This is what he is saying. The forgiveness of God is the foundation of the temple. It is the very thing on which all of what the temple stood for is based on. This blessing of forgiveness turns our midnight into morning and our sorrow into dancing. Because the forgiveness of God is given to us by the sacrifice of Christ. Are you weary because of your sin? Christ has forgiven you. Does it feel like God's discipline will never leave you? Christ has forgiven you, and all of your worship, all of your prayers, all of your offerings are accepted because they are built on the foundation of Christ's forgiveness.

The reality of the forgiveness of Christ in the face of your sin should fill your heart with joy. It should turn your heart from mourning to singing, your weeping to dancing. Let this reality fill your heart and your mind, let it calm your soul, let it move you to dance for joy with the God who forgives.

Eugene Petersen in his paraphrase of this psalm translates verses 11-12 this way,

> *You did it: you changed wild lament*
>   *into whirling dance;*
> *You ripped off my black mourning band*
>   *and decked me with wildflowers.*
> *I'm about to burst with song;*
>   *I can't keep quiet about you.*
> *G<small>OD</small>, my God,*
>   *I can't thank you enough.*†

---

* Hengstenberg, E.W., Commentary on the Psalms Vol. 1, (T&T Clark, London, 1869), 485.
† Eugene H. Peterson, *The Message: The Bible in Contemporary Language* (Colorado Springs, CO: NavPress, 2005), Psalm 30:11-12.

DAY 52

WE WILL OUT-SING THE ENEMY

By Jared C. Wilson

One of my favorite scenes in my all-time favorite movie occurs in the classic *Casablanca*, when Nazi soldiers mingle uncomfortably with the French occupants in Rick's Moroccan café. The soldiers begin singing the patriotic German anthem *"Die Wacht am Rhein,"* which sounds about as terse as the German title implies! The French, however, begin singing *"La Marsellaise."* If you haven't seen the movie, it may be difficult to hear in your mind, so I encourage you to look it up online. The scene is readily available on sites like YouTube.

The two groups begin to sing against each other, dueling as it were. The song of freedom is bubbling up within and eventually over the song of the oppressors. It is a stirring moment that gives me goosebumps every time as "La Marsellaise" eventually overcomes the soundtrack, and the resolute faces of the French singers gives the moment an even more triumphant air.

Psalm 144:7-11 is like that. The sound of our oppression, our bondage, and our shame, threatens to drown us out. It is overwhelming. The voice of the accuser, our enemy the devil, rings so loudly in our ears as it to shake our very souls. We begin to cry out ourselves to our Savior:

> **Stretch out your hand from on high; rescue me and deliver me from the many waters, from the hand of foreigners, whose mouths speak lies and whose right hand is a right hand of falsehood. (vv.7-8)**

Sometimes we fear the voice of our accuser will win the day. He mixes the truth with his lies, declaring condemnation over us for our sin. So we must sing our own song but louder still. We must shout out the good news over ourselves and each other.

> **I will sing a new song to you, O God; upon a ten-stringed harp I will play to you, who gives victory to kings, who rescues David his servant from the cruel sword. Rescue me and deliver me from the hand of foreigners, whose mouths speak lies and whose right hand is a right hand of falsehood. (vv. 9–11)**

I'm reminded of another song story. In the *Lord of the Rings* mythopoeia, Eru is the great divine being (God) who created the world through song. Before time began, he instructed the Ainur (angels) to sing a song together that would glorify him. But one of the Ainur named Melkor decided to sing his own tune, discordant to the one glorifying of Eru. Melkor was forbidden by Eru to sing his own song, but he has been trying to ever since. The enlightened beings of Middle Earth, then, look forward to the day when all is set to right once again and all beings sing Eru's song in harmony.

In our world, what is thought to be the right song is Melkor's prideful number. It is an act of holy subversion, then, to sing the song of Light into the pervasive darkness.

In the end, our enemy's song will be overcome. Take heart, friends, and let us out-sing the accuser. Our song is truer and better.

DAY 53

THE HARD AND WONDERFUL DEEDS OF GOD

By Cindy Koch

For our children.

Listen, dear one. Hear the words of the Lord. I will no longer hide these great and terrible things from you, because they are a matter of life and death. Instinctively, I want to protect you from such heavy and difficult stories. I want to keep you safe from the dark, deep wisdom who surrounds us. But you must hear, because it is who you are.

These ancient tales of miracles and wonders from a fairytale of old are only the beginning of the glorious deeds of the Lord. Perfection in a garden, deadly plagues, a stunning division of the seas, and deliverance from the enemies.

But God's people are ungrateful and unbelieving. As soon as the heavenly Father fed them, they complained and turned their backs. After the Lord Almighty delivered them from death, they wished again for bondage. After loving his people in incredibly miraculous ways, these children tested and rebelled against him.

But do you, dear child, think you are any better than the treacherous children of Israel? Taking your God for granted when he feeds and protects you. Testing and rebelling against his word when it doesn't suit your lifestyle. Compromising his great and perfect commandments when you can't meet up to the standard. No, no, dear child. You also are ungrateful and unbelieving.

No one is righteous. No one seeks after God. Everyone has turned. Everyone deserves the wrath of God. From the young baby born into a lifetime of sin to the older generation that has grown up a lifetime in the church, not one of us keeps the commandments as God gave them. All of us fall short. All of us are consigned to judgment.

> **We will not hide them from their children but tell to the coming generation the glorious deeds of the Lord, and his might, and the wonders that he has done. (Psalm 78:4)**

And so, my child, you are a miserable sinner. You have rejected and spurned the almighty God. As soon as the heavenly Father feeds you, you complain and turn your back. After the Lord Almighty delivered you from death, you now wish again for bondage. While he loves you in incredibly miraculous ways, you still test and rebel against him. This is the great and terrible story I must tell you. Because without it, you might believe something else about yourself. You might think you are strong enough to resist all temptation and do the perfect will of God. You might think your good works are enough to impress a Lord above all creation. If you do not hear the true story of your rotten and wicked heart, you might believe there is something good you have brought with you, rather than dragging the chains of sin and death.

> **For while we were still weak, at the right time Christ died for the ungodly. For one will scarcely die for a righteous person—though perhaps for a good person one would dare even to die—but God shows his love for us in that while we were still sinners, Christ died for us. (Romans 5:6-8)**

But there is so much more, dear child. Just as in the tales of old, the almighty Lord still does great and wonderful things. And his actions are always for a purpose. He comes down from the highest heavens, touching his creation for you. Since there is nothing you can do but run away, God acts for you. God made flesh bled on the cross instead of you. Death and shame have been destroyed on your behalf. God accepted Christ's payment so that you now are assured of eternal life.

His action is for the salvation of his people. Time and time again, God seeks out his own broken sinners. But he has always been working for your benefit, caring for his own dear children.

I know it is hard to hear the words of the Lord, that you have less than nothing that is righteous before God—that you work and only produce sin and failure and that you desire evil instead of good. Even though it is hard, I will no longer hide these great and terrible things from you. I cannot protect you from the difficult and heavy stories, because they are part of you. Without the beginning of the severe and needful story, you might believe there is not a complete and comforting end.

Even if I lied to you about the devastating truth of your identity, I can't keep you away from the incredible wisdom that surrounds us. Our wonderful God will continually chase you with his mercy, pursuing you with his word, stalking you with his gifts. Even now when you least deserve it, he killed his Son so that you will live. The mercy of God has and will never let you go. Dear child, you must hear, because this is who you are.

DAY 54

WHAT A MADMAN TEACHES US ABOUT PRAYER IN CHAOTIC TIMES

By Chad Bird

In the most chaotic times of life, we maintain a white-knuckled grip on anything that remains predictable. It might be a close friendship or a gym routine. It might be something simple like how you fold and stack the towels. This is not OCD. It's clinging to a vestige of stability. Unchangeableness. Something or someone to anchor us while we're whirling in a vortex of uncertainty.

If that's you, I get it. I've been there, lots of times. If your health, career, or marriage feels like one of those vomit-inducing carnival rides, the last thing you need is more of your life unhinged. I have a suggestion. It might sound strange, but hear me out.

I got the idea from a madman.

There was once an outlaw who hid in a town teeming with his enemies. This was risky, but so was returning home. He was hunted man. When his cover was blown, he quickly went to Plan B. He faked insanity. He scratched at the walls with his fingernails and let saliva run out of his mouth and down his beard.

When the authorities pulled the man before the king, the ruler was dismissive. "Look, I have enough madmen in my town already. I don't need one more. Away with him!" So the outlaw madman escaped. He wrote a unique prayer afterward. The madman's name is David, and his story is recorded in 1 Samuel 21:10-15. His prayer is Psalm 34.

We'd expect a prayer from such a man, in such an insanely chaotic season of life, to be barely intelligible—a hodgepodge of gibberish lines that read like the lyrics of a rap song on crack. But no, it's not. Quite the opposite.

Psalm 34 is one of a handful of acrostic psalms in the Bible. Acrostic means each line begins with the successive letter of the Hebrew alphabet: *aleph*, *bet*, *gimel*, *dalet*, and so forth, all the way to *tav*. If we were to imitate it in (somewhat wooden) English, the lines would go something like this:

[A] At all times I will bless the Lord . . .

[B] Boasting in the Lord is what my soul shall do . . .

[C] Come, magnify the Lord with me . . .

The psalm goes on, each line methodically, predictably following the unchangeable alphabet of the Hebrew people, from aleph to tav, A to Z.

That's interesting, you might be thinking, *but so what? How is this going to help me in my own chaotic life?*

It seems to me that there is an unspoken but vital truth in this prayer. The more out of control our lives becomes, the more stable and predictable prayers can be. You may feel like throwing a fit and basically coming unhinged before God. If so, go for it. I've done that too—amens amalgamated with tears and snot and profanity. Thank God he's got thick skin and a big heart. But we need more than a release valve for stress. We need methodical, predictable prayers that lead us from A to B to C all the way to Z and back.

And that's what we have in psalms like this one from David.

When the disciples of Jesus asked him how to pray, he replied, "Well, you know, just say whatever's on your heart." No, actually, he didn't. He gave them the Lord's Prayer, word for word, every syllable of it. God supplied the words that God wanted them to say back to him. Isn't that how we learn a language? By repeating back what is first said to us? So it is with all biblical prayers.

The psalms are God's words to us that become our words back to God. As Dietrich Bonhoeffer writes in *Psalms: The Prayer Book of the Bible*,

> **If we are to pray aright, perhaps it is quite necessary that we pray contrary to our own heart. Not what we want to pray is important, but what God wants us to pray. If we were dependent entirely on ourselves, we would probably pray only the fourth petition of the Lord's Prayer. But God wants it otherwise.** ***The richness of the Word of God ought to determine our prayer, not the poverty of our heart.*** **(p. 14, emphasis added)***

There's some wild and untamed prayers in the psalms. But they're fenced in by order, symmetry, predictability. They organize chaos. And they bring order and hope and stability to our chaotic lives. More importantly, they bring Christ into our chaotic lives, who gallops on the back of these verses to bring peace into the midst of turmoil.

Indeed, although David wrote Psalm 34, it belongs to Jesus. It is first and foremost his prayer before it becomes David's or ours. John quotes verse 20 in reference to Jesus on the cross: "[God] keeps all his bones; not one of them is broken" (cf. John 19:36). As we pray in concert with Jesus, the crucified, we die and rise with him. We seek the Lord, and he answers us (34:4). We taste and see that he is good (v. 8). He is near to us, the brokenhearted (v. 18). And he redeems our lives as we take refuge in the life of the one who gave us his life for us, that we might have the peace that passes understanding (v. 22).

---

* Dietrich Bonhoeffer, Psalms: The Prayer Book of the Bible (Grand Rapids: Fortress Press, 1974), p. 14.

DAY 55

WHEN JESUS COMES CLOSE

By Donavon Riley

Why do the nations conspire and the peoples plot in vain?
—Psalm 2:1

David introduces this psalm by explaining that when the kingdom of God comes, it will be met with resistance. Whole nations will conspire against God's Christ. People will dream up useless plots to silence the gospel. Nations, authorities, and people will rise up against the Lord. But for all their efforts, nobody can hold back God's promises and gifts. So as much as we may be scared by what we witness as people try to shut up God's preachers, all their efforts are for nothing. God will send his preachers, the gospel will be proclaimed, and his gifts will be showered upon his chosen people. What they do not understand is that when they persecute, slander, and tear down what God has set in place, it is not us who they attack but the Lord. That is why David begins this psalm by pointing us to hope and comfort, to turn us toward our Savior God rather than the fear and hopelessness the world inspires.

We see every day how earthly rulers and authorities attack the gospel. They point at all the evil done in the name of God, how wars and revolutions and genocide have been perpetrated under cover of serving a higher good. Family and friends delight in alerting us to the divisions and disagreements among the churches, and the immorality and vices of so-called "good Christian people." Of course, what they say is true. The church is full of sinners, who commit horrible, condemnable acts in the name of God. But what they cannot comprehend is that despite what sinners do, God's kingdom still comes to us. God's Word is still our incarnate Savior. The cross of Jesus stands over the wrecks of time no matter how much force, power, and violence is thrown at it, whether from within or outside the church.

But listen to what the Holy Spirit teaches us in this psalm. The nations will rage and roar, sinners will continue to sin, and the people will go on in its rebellion regardless of Jesus's death and resurrection. This does not mean God is powerless or the gospel is of no effect. Instead, when God's kingdom comes, and the gospel is preached, rebellion is our natural reaction. Against whom? Against the Lord and his Christ. Whenever God speaks his promise, wars will erupt, rulers will conspire against the Lord's preachers, and people will plot and conspire to discredit and drive us away from the gospel.

And so, we confess in the face of so much opposition and violence: "Even though God's kingdom appears to be a weak and needy thing, and the gospel powerless to effect change and God's people seem to be no better than the people who accuse them of high hypocrisy and selfishness, that does not, therefore, mean God and his promises are worthless." The Jews pleaded with Pilate to execute Jesus, and so in the end, he relented and did what they asked. Does this mean, since Jesus did not save himself from suffering and death, that he is not the Christ? Of course not. What does it matter to our Lord what people think of how he chooses to save us from sin and death? This way of thinking points to the perverse way we imagine God must affect our salvation, by earthly power and force. But if we are not willing to believe that the Son of God wins the kingdom for us by losing, we stumble into the same crowd that plots and conspires against our Savior.

This is why the first verse of this psalm serves to teach us that when God's kingdom comes when the gospel is preached, it is met by hostility and rebellion against the Lord and his Christ. This is also what Jesus explains in the gospel (Luke 11:21-22) when he warns that Satan is a well-armed man who rules in such a way that his house is always safe, secure, and at peace. But when the stronger man comes, then Satan and his whole household rage and do everything they can to push back the stronger man. Satan hates God's Christ, his promise, and his gifts. So, when Jesus comes close, Satan, nations, and peoples will close in around him and try to drive him away. But no matter what they may do, they cannot overcome our Savior. Our Lord remains steadfast for us, and even though the whole of hell and earth rise up against God and his chosen people, nothing can separate us from him, his kingdom, and his gospel. Nothing can separate us from the love of God in Jesus Christ.

DAY 56

YOU ARE WELCOME HERE

By Elyse Fitzpatrick

But I, through the abundance of your steadfast love, will enter your house.
—Psalm 5:7

What do you think God's disposition is toward you? Sure, if you've had a great day, checked off everything on your spiritual to-do list, spoken kindly to the barista who got your coffee order wrong, and helped your neighbor bring in his trash cans, you might think: *God's pretty happy with me. In fact, he's probably pretty lucky to have someone who represents him so well like me.* It's easy to think that the Lord will welcome you in when all your ducks are in a row, right? But how do you feel when you've had a terrible day, didn't want to pray or read so you blew it off, shamed the barista because getting a simple coffee drink right really isn't brain surgery, and felt a little glee when you saw your neighbor's trash can being blown down the street? Will you be welcome in God's house then?

In this psalm, David asks the Lord to lead him in righteousness and then contrasts the difference between those who are evil and those who are good . . . and God's disposition toward them. If we read this psalm without knowing anything about the gospel, we're likely to conclude that there are days when God hates us and doesn't want to be around us. "The boastful shall not stand before your eyes," David wrote. "You hate all evildoers" (v. 5). Did you see that? How are we supposed to read these words? How can we have courage to cry to the Lord (v. 2) or "prepare a sacrifice" (v. 3) for him, when we know that there is a good possibility that he probably hates us (at least part of the time)? How dare we waltz into church on the Lord's day, knowing how he feels about us?

Since the summer of 1971, I've been entering the house of the Lord, the church, pretty much every Sunday. Of course, there were times when I thought I really had done a nice job of being Mrs. Christianity because I hadn't thought much about the law that week at all. But then there were other days, days when I knew I hadn't done what I should have done and had cavalierly done what I shouldn't have done. How, if I had any self-awareness at all, or even a drop of honesty, can I walk into the house of an infinite being who knows me intimately and probably hates me? And why would I even want to? After all, if I know that someone really despises me, why would I want to be around him or her? Why would he or she want to be around me?

We begin to understand how to sing this song when we consider verse 7, "But I, through the abundance of your steadfast love, will enter your house." I can only enter into the Lord's house through the abundance of his "steadfast love." How do I dare to walk into his presence? Only by his abundant, steadfast love. He has a ridiculous, overflowing, more than adequate amount of steadfast love for you and me. Steadfast love in the Hebrew is the word *hesed*, which "is a kind of love, including mercy" for people "in a pitiful state."* Thank God for his steadfast, kind, merciful love!

In our continual struggle against sin, the Lord takes pity all who know they can who take refuge in him and do so, rather than in their own goodness. When you come into the house of the Lord, you're not coming in because you've had what you might call a "good week." No, you're accepted there because God loves to pour his mercy out on all who "take refuge in him" (v. 11). Everyone who flees to Jesus, his forgiveness, and his imputed righteousness, everyone who knows that

---

* R. Laird Harris, "698 חסד," ed. R. Laird Harris, Gleason L. Archer Jr., and Bruce K. Waltke, *Theological Wordbook of the Old Testament* (Chicago: Moody Press, 1999), 307.

they're not bringing anything that might atone for their own failures are welcomed there. As nineteenth-century pastor Charles Spurgeon preached,

> **You, Miss Much-afraid, over yonder, you are to rejoice! You, Mr. Despondency, hardly daring to look up, you must yet learn to sing. As for Mr. Ready-to-halt, he must dance on his crutches, and Feeble-mind must play the music for him.***

Don't let your fear stop you from rejoicing in his house. Don't let your sadness or depression keep you from singing of his mercy. Throw your weakness away from you and delight in this fact: God loves to welcome sinners into his house. Why? Simply because he derives pleasure from being merciful. Don't walk in remembering your past: God has forgiven you. As for the present, the Lord who loves you is with you, and as you consider the future, he has promised to be with you because of his steadfast love, mercy, and kindness. Rejoice in his house—you're not going there to prove your great faithful service to him. No, you're going there to allow him to serve you, with his word and his meal. Rejoice and know you are welcomed here.

---

* C. H. Spurgeon, "Joy, Joy for Ever," in *The Metropolitan Tabernacle Pulpit Sermons*, vol. 36 (London: Passmore & Alabaster, 1890), 290.

DAY 57

JESUS AND TROUBLED WATERS

By Erick Sorensen

The Lord *upholds all who are falling and*
raises up all who are bowed down.
—Psalm 145:14

In 1970, Paul Simon of Simon & Garfunkel released the song "Bridge Over Troubled Water." By many people's accounts, it's one of the most beautiful songs to come out of that period.

> **I'm on your side, oh, when times get rough, and friends just can't be found. Like a bridge over troubled water, I will lay me down.**

Simon wrote that song to his wife. He wrote those promises to her. But sadly, five years later they were divorced.

If we're honest, in spite of our good intentions to really be there for people, to stick with them "no matter what," to love them "unconditionally," our story often ends up the same. Hopefully it's not our marriage that buckles under the pressure like Simon's, but give us enough time, and we're bound to let somebody down. At some point, we all collapse under the weight of those who are falling and who are bowed down.

At the same time, this reality is true for those we look to for strength. Yes, we can look to them for help, and yes it's good to have friends in our struggles, but ultimately we cannot expect anyone on this planet to at all times have the strength, the perseverance, and the faithfulness to "uphold us" when we're falling and to "raise us up" when we are bowed down.

Why is this? Because this is explicitly the work of the Lord of heaven and earth. If we look to another to be this "Bridge over the troubled waters" of our lives (and vice versa), we are expecting them to do something only God can do for us.

So we look to the Lord, the true Bridge over the troubled waters of our lives. Only he has the power to heal every disease. Only he can raise the dead, to create out of nothing. Only he has the strength to carry all our sins to the cross. Only he has the power to declare sinners into saints. And only he can promise to lift up those who are broken and bowed down and make good on his word.

Yes, God is faithful to the very ones we can't handle: the poor in spirit, the weak, the needy, the helpless addicts, the seemingly useless ones. In other words, God is faithful *to us* because all have "fallen" and have been "boweddown" (whether it's due to our own sin and fallenness or just merely being a member of a sinful and fallen world, no one's unaffected, Romans 3:23).

For example, the apostle Paul was going through a mighty struggle in his life. He had what he referred to as a thorn in his side that just wouldn't go away (Was it a specific sin he struggled with? Or was it a physical or mental ailment?) What that thorn was, only God and Paul know, but we do know this thorn had caused Paul to fall and be brought low. So three times he pleaded with the Lord to take away this terrible problem. Surely, if anyone's prayer for deliverance and healing would be answered, it would be the mighty apostle Paul's. But God said to him famously, "My grace is sufficient for you, for my power is made perfect in weakness" (2 Corinthians 12:8).

Yes, even when he doesn't take away the "troubled waters" of our life, he is the Bridge we can lean on no matter what storms may come our way.

So take heart and remember the same one who commands the waves to be still says to you today, "Come to me, all who labor and are heavy laden, and I will give you rest" (Matthew 11:28).

DAY 58

FORGET NOT ALL HIS BENEFITS

By Jessica Thompson

I have the easiest time remembering all the good things I have done. How I was kind in the face of anger. How I gave to the needy. How I rarely miss the Sunday gathering. How I have had a quiet time four days in a row and have actually looked forward to it. How I spent that one summer decades ago living in an orphanage serving those kids. How I sent a text to that one friend who I knew was struggling. On and on the list of my goodness goes, and on and on I love rehearsing that list before myself so I don't forget all my benefits.

I also have the easiest time remembering all of my failures. How I was impatient when one of my kids just wanted to talk. How I ignored the needs of my community because a new pair of boots seemed like a better idea. How I went to the Sunday gathering out of obligation and felt absolutely nothing for God when I heard that my sins were forgiven. How I went for weeks and months without even thinking of spending any time with my Jesus and didn't even care that my heart was cold. How I spend days bingeing anything on Netflix to numb my heart and mind to pain. How I neglected to send any texts or return any emails from friends who were hurting and asking for prayer. On and on the list of my badness goes, and on and on I find myself rehearsing it.

And then this gem of a verse makes it way through the darkness of my thought life and presents itself to me in all of its glory. *"Bless the Lord, Oh my soul, and forget not all of his benefits"* (Psalm 103:3).

Remember him. David had to tell himself, we have to tell ourselves, don't forget who he is and what he has done.

He forgives all your sins. Every single one. Forgiven. He doesn't just forgive sins generally speaking. He forgives all of *our* personal sins. Every single sin where we use our goodness as a way to avoid needing him. Every single sin that causes us to look to other loves besides him. Every sin of inflated opinion of self. Every sin of ignoring someone in need. Every time we look with self-righteous judgment on the sins of others. Every time we are sure that we understand grace more than the next guy and somehow that makes us a better Christian. Every single sin from our past that causes shame to burn in our chest when we think about it. Every time we use whatever and whoever is necessary to advance self. Every single sin we are hiding and loving right this second. Every single horrific sin we will commit in the future. All of it. It is all forgiven. Scandalous grace how sweet the sound that saves wretches like us.

He heals all our diseases. Every single disease of unbelief finds its healing in the wounds of our Savior. *"He heals your faithlessness"* (Jeremiah 3:22). *"I will heal their apostasy; I will love them freely"* (Hosea 14:4). He heals our apostasy, our very abandonment and renunciation of our faith. He takes that unto himself, and he heals it. He heals our faithlessness. Every time you and I chose to believe lies instead of believing his love for us, he takes that unto himself and heals us. His love knows no bounds. He heals the brokenhearted, even if that broken heart is a result of our own sin. He is the Lord our healer.

Victor Hugo says, "The supreme happiness of life is the conviction that we are loved; love for ourselves—say rather, loved in spite of ourselves."* Forget not his benefits, beloved. Rehearse his eternal love for you. Rehearse his healings. He has redeemed your life from the pit. He crowns us with steadfast love and mercy. He satisfies us with good things. He is merciful and gracious, slow to anger, and abounding in unmovable love. He does not deal with us according to our sins. He doesn't repay us according to all of the moral debt we have accrued. Go outside today and look up. *"For as high as the heavens are*

---

* Victor Hugo, *Les Miserables*, Public Domain.

above the hearth, so great is his steadfast love toward those who fear him" (Psalm 103:11). Go outside today and look from the east to the west. *"As far as the east is from the west, so far does he remove our transgressions from us"* (Psalm 103:12). Find supreme happiness in being loved in spite of all of your brokenness. That happiness is there for you right this second. He is there for you right this second.

DAY 59

WELCOME HOME

By Donavon Riley

Blessed is he who comes in the name of the Lord!
We bless you from the house of the LORD.
—Psalm 118:26

Although it is easy to become confused, the gospel is not about Jesus. The gospel is Jesus Christ. The "good news," as the Bible puts it, is a present tense announcement that Jesus is "for you." He is actually present "for you" when a preacher speaks the words that deliver Jesus for the forgiveness of sin, life, and eternal salvation. Or to put it another way, when we are in love, we do not ask the beloved, "Please describe what love means to you." Instead, we say to the beloved, "I love you."

The gospel works in a similar way. God does not ask us, "What does the good news about Jesus mean to you?" Instead, our heavenly Father sends a preacher with a specific message that delivers what it declares: "For Christ's sake you are forgiven." God speaks, and what he says happens. For example, when God says, "Let there be light," there is light. Likewise, when the Father says, "You are forgiven for Jesus's sake," it happens. He no longer recalls our sin. He does not remember our sin anymore because now all he sees when he looks at us is the blood of his Son, which covers us. All the Father sees is his Son standing in front of us, as our mediator, "our own high priest," as Paul writes in his letter to the Hebrews.

What we imagine the gospel is and is not, whatever we teach about the gospel having something to do with our works, intentions, or feelings, none of them are "good news." When we confuse our doing for God with the Father's doing for us, we end up preaching the worst bad news message of all. We end up, it turns out, rejecting the gospel, and therefore we reject Jesus.

When we insist on injecting our own meaning into the gospel, we will inevitably say to God's preacher, "Get away from us, you devil! Why are you trying to tempt us and lead us into sin?" On the other hand, anyone caught by the gospel says, "Blessed is he who comes in the name of the Lord!"

The gospel preached, Jesus delivering himself to us in simple, earthly words, also leads us to sing, "We bless you from the house of the Lord!" God's good words inspire us. His gospel-breathed word delivers to us exactly what it preaches. The gospel draws out of us, not questions about meaning, but words of thanks, praise, happiness, and joy because we are told the good news: "For Christ's sake you are counted as residents in the house of the Lord. You are not strangers to God. You are not tourists. You are members of his household today and always."

The gospel is built on the rejected cornerstone. What we imagine the good news of Jesus Christ means does not matter. All that matters, even when we demand a gospel that meets our self-serving needs, is that Jesus comes to us as Giver and Gift through the message of his preacher. The preacher's message is the Father's own word, and the same message the angels, the saints in every generation, and all creatures proclaim. On account of this, as the psalmist writes, the house of the Lord is wherever the gospel is preached because where the good news is proclaimed, our heavenly Father is there with his Christ. On the other hand, where the gospel is not preached, God is not there.

Where the gospel is spoken, God's house erupts with songs and prayers of grace and life and joy, even though Christians may be suffering and afflicted. And as our Lord says, "In every place where I cause my name [that is, my word] to be remembered I will come to you and bless you" (Exodus 20:24). Wherever our Father sends his preacher to deliver the message of Christ's salvation, his name and his work will be celebrated. The gospel preached also brings with it limitless grace and immeasurable blessing. That is why the scripture refers to the gospel as good news.

We enter into the house of the Lord because we have been declared residents of his house. It is for Christians, it turns out, the only place in this world where we can take comfort in knowing it is the only house where we truly belong and are accepted unconditionally, warts and messes and scars and all. The gospel belongs to Jesus Christ. The gospel is Jesus Christ given "for you." When he comes to us, we do not have to worry about what it means to us because when our Lord speaks to us, he does what he says, declaring us forgiven of all sin, blessed, and firmly set as a resident in the house of the Lord.

DAY 60

A HELMET OF PROMISES

By Bruce Hillman

---

*O LORD, my Lord, the strength of my salvation,
you have covered my head in the day of battle.
—Psalm 140:7*

One of the most troubling days in my life happened in my first semester of college in a Western Civilization class. The class topics covered the Old and New Testament eras, and being a lifelong Christian, I assumed these areas would be of little difficulty for me. What an arrogant assumption!

When the professor got to the sections about Jesus and our primary source of knowledge about him (the Bible), the professor proceeded to show all the apparent contradictions and supposed inconsistencies that inferred a flawed and untrustworthy book. As the professor began to compare verses that seemed to blatantly contradict one another, I began to feel sick. I remember getting in my car to go home after class and feeling completely lost. For the first time in my life, my bubble had been burst. I had always heard objections to the logic or morality of Christianity, but this was the first time I heard the very source of revelation, the Bible, was self-contradicting. I began to wonder if everything I had believed my whole life was wrong. If the Bible was untrustworthy, how could I know anything or maintain my faith? I felt like the ground was swept out from under me, and I was unmoored, floating in an abyss of confusion and having nothing else to grab hold of to give life meaning or purpose. It was dreadful.

In the long run, the professor did me a favor. By bursting my bubble, he inspired me to seek out answers to questions about my faith that I might not have otherwise asked. But the process was painful, difficult, and full of doubts. I had always believed in the power of faith, but that professor also showed me its fragility.

In this verse, we hear of a very fragile part of the body—the head. In the violence of battle, the head must be protected by a helmet, for if you strike a man's leg, shoulder, or arm, he might still fight, but cut into his head and his whole body is done. So the head must be protected at all costs. The problem is, if you were to fight so defensively that you always attempted to protect your head, you wouldn't fight well. A helmet does the work of defense for you so that you can concentrate on your enemies.

In this verse, we hear an amazing promise—in essence, that God is your helmet. Specifically, this helmet is your salvation. Not only is the Lord himself your salvation (Psalm 27:1), but he is also the *strength* of your salvation. *Your* Lord takes responsibility for *your* salvation. It both comes and is sustained by God's own hand. And we hear this type of assurance many times, such as in the famous benediction, "May the Lord bless you and keep you" (Numbers 6:24). He will be your helmet. He will be your salvation and the quality of that salvation.

When my professor attempted to undermine the authority of God's word, I was terrified I might have lost my salvation. I even wondered if there was any salvation at all. But what I have come to see is that while anyone can make a conscious decision to walk away from God or deny him, a person can't accidentally lose his or her salvation. Why? Because God preserves it. He is faith's strength. He will bless and keep. He will be for us what we cannot be. He will give to us what we do not have. He will sustain us beyond our abilities.

In the many dark nights that the faithful bear, we must not lose heart. The enemy will lash and strike, the flesh will doubt and argue, but God will be the helmet shielding us from ultimate harm.

Having such a great defense, then, let's go to work on the real battle: telling others about Jesus, loving our neighbors, and doing the work of the kingdom. And remember, God himself promises to be *your* God and *your* strength. Let us live in this promise.

MEET THE AUTHORS

ERICK SORENSEN is married to Melissa and they have 3 boys together. He is the pastor of Epiphany Lutheran Church in Manhattan. He earned his Master of Divinity Degree from Lutheran Brethren Seminary. He is a Christ Hold Fast Contributor, co-host of the podcast *30 Minutes in the New Testament*, and serves as the Chairman of *Fifth Act Church Planting*.

DONAVON RILEY is a Lutheran pastor, conference speaker, author, Online Content Director for Higher Things, a contributing writer at 1517, Christ Hold Fast, and LOGIA. He is pastor of Saint John Lutheran Church in Webster, MN. A graduate of Concordia Universities in St. Paul, Minnesota and Portland, Oregon, Pastor Riley received his seminary and post-graduate education at Luther Seminary in St. Paul, Minnesota. He is married to Annie, and is the father of four children.

BRUCE HILLMAN is Lead Pastor at Hillside Lutheran Brethren Church in Succasunna New Jersey. He Holds a BA in History and Political Science from Quinnipiac University, (Hamden, CT), an MDiv. from the Lutheran Brethren Seminary (Fergus Falls, MN) and an STM in Patristics from Drew University (Madison, NJ); his research involves Augustinian studies and Early Christianity. He is co-founder of *Fifth Act Church Planting*.

DANIEL EMERY PRICE is the Director of Christ Hold Fast. He is an author, church and conference speaker, cohost of the podcasts *40 Minutes in the Old Testament* and *30 Minutes in the New Testament*, and he leads the interactive online *Bible Study For Normies*. Daniel has served as a church planter, pastor and worship leader and currently lives in Bentonville, Arkansas, with his wife Jessica and daughter Anna.

CHAD BIRD is an author and speaker devoted to honest Christianity that addresses the raw realities of life. The Gospel is for broken, messed up people like himself. He has served as an assistant professor of OT theology, contributed hymns to the Lutheran Service Book, and cohosts the podcast *40 Minutes in the Old Testament*. He holds Master's degrees from Concordia Theological Seminary and Hebrew Union College. He has contributed articles to Modern Reformation, The Federalist, Concordia Pulpit Resources, The Gospel Coalition, Mockingbird and other journals and websites. He is the author of the books *Night Driving: Notes from a Prodigal Soul* and *Your God Is Too Glorious*. Chad and his wife, Stacy, have four children and two grandchildren together and live in the Texas Hill Country.

JESSICA THOMPSON has authored or coauthored several books, including the bestseller *Give Them Grace*. She is a conference speaker, blogger and co-host of the podcast *Front Porch with the Fitzes*. She lives in Southern California with her husband and their three teenage children.

DANIEL VAN VOORHIS is the director of the *League of Faithful Masks*, scholar-in-residence and director of curriculum at 1517. After receiving his PhD in Modern history from the University of St. Andrews, Dr. van Voorhis spent 11 years teaching history and political thought at Concordia University, Irvine and was most recently the assistant Dean of the School of Arts and Sciences. Dr. van Voorhis has published articles and chapters in books on subjects ranging from the Reformation to the Enlightenment and Cold War. He speaks nationally in academic and general conference settings. He is currently the co-host of the *Virtue in the Wasteland* podcast and the author of the book *Monsters*.

ELYSE FITZPATRICK holds a certificate in biblical counseling from CCEF (San Diego) and an M.A. in Biblical Counseling from Trinity Theological Seminary. She has authored over 23 books on daily living and the Christian life. She is the co-host of the podcast *Front Porch with the Fitzes*. She is a frequent speaker at Christian conferences, she has been married for over 40 years and has three adult children and six really adorable grandchildren.

STEVEN PAULSON joined the Luther Seminary faculty as associate professor of systematic theology in the fall of 1998 after serving as assistant professor of religion at Concordia College in Moorhead, Minn., where he had been since 1993. He was pastor of Trinity Lutheran Church in Washington Island, Wis., from 1990 to 1993. His experience also includes two years of work as a research librarian at JKM Library in Chicago and five years as a psychiatric counselor at Fairview Hospitals in Minneapolis. Paulson is a Summa Cum Laude and Phi Beta Kappa graduate of St. Olaf College, Northfield, Minn., and earned the master of divinity degree from Luther Seminary in 1984. He holds both the master of theology (1988) and doctor of theology (1992) degrees from Lutheran School of Theology in Chicago.

JARED C. WILSON is the author of many books including *Gospel Wakefulness* and *The Imperfect Disciple*. He is the Director of Content Strategy for Midwestern Baptist Theological Seminary, Managing Editor of For The Church and host of the *FTC Podcast*, and Director of The Pastoral Training Center at Liberty Baptist Church in Kansas City, MO.

CINDY KOCH is wife to Pastor Paul Koch and mother of five busy children in Ventura, California. In between homeschool and church events, she writes for *1517* and *The Jagged Word*. She is a conference speaker and has an M.A. from Concordia Seminary St. Louis in exegetical theology.

JOEL FITZPATRICK has served as an ordained minister in the Presbyterian Church in America with a focus on youth and family. He received MDiv from Westminster Seminary California. He is the coauthor of the book *Mom, Dad . . . What's Sex?* and the co-host of the podcast *Front Porch with the Fitzes*. He lives in Southern California with his wife and their two children.

www.ingramcontent.com/pod-product-compliance
Lightning Source LLC
LaVergne TN
LVHW041334080426
835512LV00006B/442